Brand
Revolution

Ousting Old Mideast Trading Mindsets

Said Aghil Baaghil

iUniverse, Inc.
Bloomington

Brand Revolution
Ousting Old Mideast Trading Mindsets

iUniverse books may be ordered through booksellers or by contacting:

iUniverse
1663 Liberty Drive
Bloomington, IN 47403
www.iuniverse.com
1-800-Authors (1-800-288-4677)

ISBN: 978-1-4697-3252-7 (sc)
ISBN: 978-1-4697-3251-0 (hc)
ISBN: 978-1-4697-3250-3 (e)

Library of Congress Control Number: 2012900177

Printed in the United States of America

iUniverse rev. date: 1/3/2012

*I dedicate this book to my son Rakan Said Baaghil, and to all the
people who have made such a great difference in my life.*

*A special dedication to
King Abdullah bin Abdul-Aziz Al Saud of Saudi Arabia: I love you for
all the great things you have done. I consider you the true leader of
the Arab world—May god bless you all the way*

*Special Thanks:
To Saudi Arabia, a place where I have truly excelled in my career and
To all my fans who have followed my work on brand marketing over
the past seven years—I love you!*

*My special thanks also go to my editor, Dr. Jody Bilyeu, who spent
great deal of time helping me form and shape my thoughts. I also a
debt of gratitude to a dear friend of mine, Moniza Khokhar, publisher
of elan, she is just an incredible person who works hard to make this
world a beautiful place.*

This book was edited by
Dr. Jody Bilyeu

Contents

Chapter 1:
A Time for Revolution

With the astounding current transformations in the worlds of politics, economy and culture, a wave of change has swept most countries around the world, from Tahrir square to the protests on Wall Street in New York. The young people spreading their new ideas using modern technologies, especially social media, have served as the main beacon of change, especially in regions such as the Middle East, where many young people had been living all their lives under corrupt dictators. Today most young people in the region are driven by hope, ambition and admiration for this unprecedented change that has brought their souls to the brink of a new frontier, crafted by their own hands, unlike previous generations whose thoughts were encoded and dictated by an education system that was conceived by those same corrupt leaders. These leaders were corrupted by their own power as well as by their greed, and they were corrupted by the dishonesty they were willing to perpetrate to cling to that power. It was in their interest that the populations of these nations would think uniformly.

And when we say they were dishonest, we mean they were putting forward occasional intentional falsehoods, certainly. But more importantly, they were in the grips of a more pernicious kind of dishonesty—self-dishonesty—in which one refuses to acknowledge the truth because one cannot acknowledge the truth, or one will have to change. And more than anything, these leaders, who after all had all they need, and had it pretty good, did not want change. In answer, the young people who have helped bring these leaders down have set transparency and honesty as central values.

Meanwhile, it must be acknowledged that the political revolution was a social revolution, and that the social revolution also entailed revolutions in such economic details as the way people consume media and products, and the way they share information about those media and products. It goes without saying that Facebook and Twitter first rose to prominence in the world, not as a vehicles for revolution, but as money-making enterprises. Yet something about *this* form of money-making was more amenable to all kinds of progress: political, social, and commercial. In today's world the three are intimately bound together, as they always have been. Yet perhaps today we are in a better position to admit to ourselves how these areas of endeavor are related, and must be related. Social responsibility now extends to consumption, and our means of consumption are now acknowledged to impact social responsibility. In one sense, the deposed leaders represented not only outmoded and morally suspect means of governance, but they also represented outmoded and morally suspect means of consumption.

Herein, when we position brand revolution in the context of this broader change, this is not to say that we consider the two areas of endeavor to be of equal importance. However, it is to say that one cannot exist without the other. The political revolution was predicated on shifting commercial paradigms. Thus, brand revolution is perhaps not the most important aspect of all this change, but it has nonetheless been vital. The claims on the part of protesters that we must find new ways of allocating resources were no less potent than their claims that we must find new ways of allocating rights and enfranchisement.

This book is about how marketing fits in to revolution, especially in the developing world, and especially the Middle East.[1] Without alleging that brand revolution is to be thought of on the same level as overthrowing a dictator, we can confidently acknowledge that changes in the way we market goods and services are part and parcel of the broader revolution, and moreover that the broader revolution could never have existed without a corresponding shift in the commercial world. It is about that shift in the commercial world that we now concern ourselves. What is brand revolution? It is the process of making room for a brand to have its own right to exist and to live in the way that best suits it.

The quest of this book is to seek change in the business environment, specifically of the Middle East region, and to acquire a new mindset and pave the way for a new generation of leaders who can lead the regional brands to a more global platform. Such change is inescapable as industries are growing and the world is becoming ever more competitive. The necessity to change how we conduct our business in order for our brands to thrive and achieve, as many companies from many other nations have continued to do, is undeniable. The question is whether any of the current menagerie of CEOs will lead that change, or whether it will instead be the new CEOs who replace the old ones upon their failure, or indeed the firms who replace their failed firms after a company-wide collapse.

As opposed to many of the companies in our region, companies in much of the world, including in much of the developing world, have branded their nations as well as their companies, and have in many cases created what appears to be everlasting love and esteem, and helped their countries to be a destination for many reasons. Today the world is conditioned by and built upon the

---

1   For the purposes of this book, the Middle East will be defined as including some parts of North Africa, and when I refer to Arabs, I will be referring to those from both East and North Africa in addition to those in the Middle East as usually defined. Such defines our current operating region and our short-term target region for discussion in this book.

fast pace of technology, yet almost everything has been simplified to handheld devices as we go about our business and arrange our daily lives. So where does the Arab world stand in the midst of these speed-driven changes? Where do our small size and our midsize companies stand in the midst of all this? Who's there to support them?

What follows are blunt words, but I believe they are all the more needful for the offense they might offer, because there is a way of doing things in our world which cannot continue, and which it will be offensive to many of us to end: Most of the business leaders in the region, CEOs, CFOs, CMOs, and COOs, have reached the positions they occupy, it must be acknowledged, merely based on favoritism.

In the midst of such a situation, there is a level of dishonesty that is so pervasive that it might be easily missed. Perhaps we pretend that these people are competent to do the jobs they're supposed to be doing because we like these people and don't like to think about the opposite. Perhaps we think the distance between our desires and the reality doesn't matter in this case. Perhaps friendships and kin bonds are more important to us than the technical or professional requirements for employment. In any of these cases, there is a distance between what we say is happening, and what is really happening. Inevitably, as we defend such decisions, there emerges a defensiveness about our choices, such that we perhaps almost come to believe we acted as we should have acted. In any case, in the information age, the age of transparency, honesty, and accountability, and in the age of intensified scrutiny of nearly every position of power, such institutionalized dishonesty cannot continue. And it is this gap between pretense and truth that we must overcome as a precondition of new ways of branding.

The corruption in the appointment of company officers is merely one example of how privilege and custom, rather than merit and necessity, now set the climate of the business world in the Arab world. How can businesses thrive and grow when the conduct of commerce is fraught through with exploitation and cronyism? How can a thriving organization seize opportunities when most people are misinformed concerning the initial steps of how they should be engaging with the business world?

Such dilemmas repeat themselves to a sickening degree in this part of the world, and the failure of most of our governments to place a higher priority on overseeing applicable laws and to penalize those who are corrupt is widespread, and indeed has been another important aspect of the corruption in the business world, which of course has been intimately intertwined with the political world. This failure of oversight and justice opens still more doors for embezzlement, whether *de facto* or overt, on the part of the current generation and future generations. Brand Revolution, therefore, is first about acknowledging this sorry state of affairs, as a first step to changing it. In the following chapter, I discuss two primary conditions the revolution must work against if the Arab business world is to survive and thrive.

Chapter 2:
The Sham CEO and the
Trader's Mindset

The Sham CEOS

The current protest of brands is first and foremost against all those CEOs who destroy every brand that has great potential for leading a healthy existence, but based on their lack of understanding of brand marketing, and of the new, more transparent and level world in which marketing takes place, their poor decisions have far-reaching and unfortunately dire consequences. The CEOs are merely representatives of a deeper problem: a tradition of cronyism and nepotism, and of pretending rather than being. The problem is that these CEOs were never really CEOs at all. Consequently, the country's businesses are simply not being managed in any professional, or even sane, sense of the word.

The problem of poor CEOs is compounded by the unbelievable number of CEOs in our region. It sometimes seems anyone and everyone is a CEO. My thesis in this regard is simple: Entrepreneurs should not be mistaken as to whether they should be the CEO of their own projects if they lack management skills. They should seek to run their operations through the first few years and then hand them over to a person skilled in management to run the new firm's day-to-day operations.

Given that practically everyone in the region seems to be a CEO, CBDO, COO and so on, even people starting with new businesses having fewer than five employees seem to be applying substantial efforts to give themselves the title of CEO and accord themselves other such honors and letters in front of their names.

Here, too the specter of implicit deception looms large. Calling yourself a CEO doesn't make you a CEO. Following up that sham by arranging your lifestyle and circumstances so that the pretense of authority you're putting on seems plausible is not building a business, dear wannabe CEO; it is a pathetic sham and a colossal waste of time that you could be pouring into actually building a business, and perhaps even adding value to the world instead of merely seeking to add value to your persona. Many CEOs are embarrassingly excited by the design of their business cards, and they strive to legitimize the title on the card, and make sure the placard of their childish production has been given out to numerous people as part of building their deception. Again we see that a creeping dishonesty for the sake of suspect motives is the beginning of the fall of the empire of lies and deceptions.

I have encountered numerous CEOs, both elected and self-claimed, and while I am sure there are a great many good CEOs in the region, I am also convinced that the majority are ruining the broth for the rest. I have encountered elected CEOs who are ego-driven and ill-informed about their position in the company, and I know that they would die to be part of the clan. I have had to sit and listen to CEOs, both elected and claimed, lie through their teeth about their achievements, and yet they are the classic example of failure, all the more so because of their pitiable efforts to continue the pretense.

Nepotism underlies much of this failure and pretense. I have known some large, viably operating plants that were doing a remarkable job regarding production, salaries and benefits. The owner of the operation, however, decided to fire the CEO and have his son operate it. After the CEO took this ill-advised action, the declining margins of the plants became clearly evident. As more firms operate under this philosophy, sooner or later the existing owner will have to find a new geographical location and identify a new target audience. Often, owners who also act as the CEO hire their own children to such posts as vice president or even to as sensitive a position as vice president of marketing. These children may or may not have the qualifications to help the company thrive and survive. All too frequently, of course, they do not, given that their qualifications were not the primary consideration in their hiring, if they were any part of the consideration at all.

Perhaps it will be useful to give some more specific example of sham CEOs. The first example is a good illustration of the problem of deception and self-deception among business leadership. There's a man in my acquaintance who owns a locally based fitness center. I listened to him lie about his supposed successes—and this was when I knew about his failure, and he knew of it, and he knew I knew of it!—and yet he still nominated himself to be the CEO of the gym and served in that role until the investors finally had to push him out when he predictably failed.

In a classic example of the harmful effects of self-deception in the Arab business world, and of the often amazing extent to which it seems to thrive, this same individual continually blames his failures on others and desperately tries to hang his problems on other people's shoulders. Once the investors pushed him out, unbelievably, he spread a rumor that his organization had merged with a leading firm in the industry. There are so many things wrong with this scenario that it is difficult to know how to begin to address it. First and foremost: Really? In the age of instant knowledge and increased transparency, there is still someone who believes he can succeed in business based on a résumé line that it would take three seconds, if that, for a prospective investor, employer or customer to check on Google? And in the age when a humiliating account of such a bald deception could spread to several thousand people within a few seconds via Facebook? Second, as to the credibility of the claim, the mergers and acquisitions market is still too primitive in the region for it to be credible. Third, this fraud of a CEO would do well to understand that his lies can only take him so far. If he wishes to succeed, when is he going to get around to actually working at his business?

Another self-claimed CEO who runs an eyewear company can serve as an example of the influence of cronyism and nepotism in business leadership. He wishes to consult young entrepreneurs concerning how to start their own businesses. The catch is, he has completely failed even to run his own operation he has operated for the past thirty years. How could he take part in such a deception, when so many lies are so deeply embedded in the process?

Another stunning example is a man who used to try to run a small financial advisory firm when a friend knocked on his door and offered him the opportunity to start an investment firm. This friend is well-connected in the right circles of the region's who's who, and the man could scarcely turn away an opportunity literally knocking at his door. He put investors together and started this organization—and yes, he managed to raise around two hundred million dollars. In the first few years the company failed even to run into a few million riyal profit, and in its fourth year the company showed only a little over 10 million riyal in earnings.

As CEO, this man cut 50 percent of the initial jobs in the firm and closed two locations that were complete flops. Yet he remains CEO until the moment of this writing. The shareholders of this organization have continually failed to realize the truth: that this company's problem is the CEO. Yet the CEO is heading into almost his fifth year, and seems to be the single person in the organization who has benefited the most in terms of his salary, perks, and whatever else, all charged to the company, including paying for his wife to fly with him. Yes, his wife works with him in the business development department, and no matter how poorly she performs, she stays on the job, and is sure to continue doing so as long as her husband remains CEO. Meanwhile, half the company that he started his term with is looking for work.

With mindsets such as I have addressed here, none of our businesses will ever be able to move outside the region's borders. Most couldn't survive; they would be like fish flopping on dry ground, trying to emerge from the water of cronyism and deception they need to survive. The business world outside the Middle East is not perfect, by any means, and it has certainly not always earned a reputation for honesty, or even for self-honesty. That said, the businesses I have seen in the Arab world are so far below the standards of transparency and accountability that underlie business elsewhere, that the experience of a sham Arab CEO trying to take his company global would wind up being an obliteration. He would be a self-satisfied, well-feathered little rooster strutting into a room full of hungry cats. The sad truth that most Arab businesses would fail to rise to the levels of transparency, accountability, and social responsibility that most companies in the rest of the world now manage to maintain, especially in light of the justified public criticism major corporations are now facing in that regard, is all the more distressing. I am sad to acknowledge that the wider business world's lows would be highs for many businesses in the Middle East.

The reality I have shared here represents only a couple of the thousands of examples I have encountered as a consultant. In my early days in this region, around 2004, I helped initiate a local food and beverage company. The owner of the company eventually became so jealous of the successes of my company that he tried to force me to hire his daughter as my assistant. That request was denied from my desk, and I eventually resigned the account. Predictably, just a few years down the line, the company closed. Now the owner always presents his situation as a management consultation problem, yet he failed in almost every company he created in the group of companies he has named. I have seen shows on Broadway before and frequented many theaters, but this event was a show beyond my expectations. I have eventually come to refer to this event, and the phenomenon of deception that underlies it, "Hollywood."

Now, I must acknowledge the right of people to be pesky about their wishes and desires, but any great wish should come through reality, and not by means of a lie. I know of a COO of a local car company, basically a dealer of German cars, for whom his title, unfortunately, is woefully far from his intelligence and competence. The title, not to mention the post, was assigned to him because he is a member of his family, and not based on his credentials. The company has now come down to its last running lines, and has already lost one of its brands as a leader in a certain category. The point here is that even if this gentleman, who by the way dresses funny, was a family member of mine, and yet lacked the credentials for his job, I would fire him on the spot and hire someone with the actual qualifications to do the job. I think it is important to note that I would do this not only because to do so would be in the best interests of the company, but also because in reality to do so would be in the best interests of the family, to protect the family's stake in the business. I would argue, too, that ultimately removing this man from a job at which he's flailing while pretending to succeed would be in his own best interests. To pretend to be successful is worse than to fail outright, not only because perpetual dishonesty is no condition under which to live one's life, but also because the pretense of success prevents acknowledging failure. Without acknowledging failure, one can never enjoy actual success, because success must always be based on lessons learned.

Because there has yet to be acknowledgment, numerous businesses in the Arab region are continuing to fail and shut down, largely because of cronyism, inauthenticity, underqualification, and pretense. There may be some who would say businesses such as the ones I've discussed are at least commercially viable on a low level, but I'll say that at the very least, they have never served their fuller purpose of making a collective impact on the region. The region is presently individually driven, and not collectively, and few perceive the baleful effect of this self-serving single-mindedness. This resistance to acknowledgment of the facts on the ground, and of what we must do to improve is what keeps the national effort to the minimum of its growth potential.

The Trader's Mindset

The second major problem that any revolution must work against is a certain legacy of the business tradition of the region, which I'll refer to as the trader's mindset. This problem is no less important, but it's one with which I have a bit more sympathy than for the hopelessly fake CEOs whom I watch ruin the businesses of our region every day. I'm more sympathetic because this problem has to do with continuing ancient traditions bound up in honor.

As Arabs, we were the first people to trade between countries for commodities. Out of the Arab world came the Hadramis from Hadramout. They traveled to trade out of the Arabian peninsula, going as far east as Indonesia, and as far west as east Africa. That method of transaction still exists intact; in fact, it forms the majority of business operations in the Arab world today. The generic business of trading allows business owners to buy products or services and sell them to the local market or within the market as a form of product exchange. This method of business transaction is as important now as it ever was in the past in our region.

While *trading and selling* became ingrained behaviors, *producing* was never a substantial part of the Arab cultural heritage. To this day, we have minimal industry and manufacturing, and produce our own brands only very sparsely. We do, however, tend to form major mergers with foreign firms. This is a bilateral trade exchange, however, and I believe in these arrangements the foreign partner is the chief financial beneficiary. I say this because the merger partners tend to have management strategies that include globalization, with the goal of establishing a presence in almost every country with economic purchasing power. Such a strategy seeks to accomplish globalization via mergers with local operating firms. The local firm benefits by learning the trade, but not by gaining potential penetration outside its area. Trade marketing to me, therefore, is simply product dumping with a fancy name, even though the local firm may be a licensed representative of the brand within the country. This phenomenon is not a bad thing, necessarily, if the local firm's basic interest is in gaining financial benefit from its international brand within its home country. But at the end of the day, that local firm remains merely a contracted representative of the brand.

It must be said that we have been traders in the Arabian Peninsula since the time of our forefathers. This may mean that while we're perfectly willing to assay trials to make money, our horse-trading and tinker's cart mentality still sometimes rules the day, such that a cash-based or buy-and-sell mindset still runs in our business bloodline. We appear to be reluctant to leave that tradition behind. Meanwhile, the world is rolling along at a breathtaking pace to find ways to serve consumer needs more innovatively day by day, and we remain at the back of the pack trying to figure out entrepreneurship, without having our fundamentals in place, quibbling over the price of a fig instead of figuring out how to market figs in the global economy.

Chapter 3:
Our Market Reality

A growing concern among those of us who keep a close watch on the business world of the Middle East is that most firms in our region are small-scale, and even under proper development, their growth has been stagnant for a number of years. Some of the problems may be purely a result of the global economic downturn, but undoubtedly much of the stagnation may be attributed to the owner or CEO who will not change his management style or adapt to global trends of business practice, and particularly those CEOs who do not allow the marketing and finance departments to play their respective roles in the organization. Overall, these companies are in dire need of an overall structure, with a stated mission and vision for both short- and long-term growth.

How many of our brands are represented in other countries? We can certainly name a few. But having merely "a few" doesn't help our future growth in business maturity. To have Middle Eastern brands represented in other countries is a vital aspect of trade, just as much as being prominent in our regional markets. On the bright side, countries like the United Arab Emirates and Egypt have seen tremendous recent growth by means of deploying properly structured business organizations, both in the region and in the international arena.

Of successful Middle Eastern brands, let's take, for example, Orascom Telecom. Headquartered in Egypt, Orascom Telecom is a reputable mobile telecommunication operations company, both in the region and beyond. This firm's initial contact with mobile operating experience arose when the Egyptian government decided to privatize its mobile-based company. Mr. Naguib Sawiris, CEO of Orascom, won the bid and thankfully offered a stated vision for operating in a number of countries in the region. Today, Orascom operates in many countries, reaching as far as Pakistan, and its future continues to look bright. Another example, Vodafone, is based in the United Kingdom and can lay claim to being the largest mobile network company in the world. The brand exists in most Middle Eastern countries, as well as in Europe and the Far East. The company's CEO and management have a global strategy: what they sell is the brand name and their expertise. In fact, Vodafone recently merged with a locally operating mobile company in Turkey and was in a position to insist that the brand name in this region be changed to Vodafone.

These examples show that our potential in terms of branding and marketing is enormous, but the fact remains that without the proper structure and operating principles, a company is doomed to fail. Subsequent chapters of this book will explain how business owners must recognize the potential of the region; hire the right employees for the organization; and build and structure their firms to flourish in the local market, then regionally and then globally. A business owner's firm must have an adequate plan for deploying all its strategies whether those concern marketing or financing.

Taking these simple steps will change the nature of doing business in our region. These are proven models, which have worked for other companies in the region, and these changes must be made from the roots up in terms of how we conduct business today. For example, many grocery and clothing stores are individually owned, with some constituting chains that represent imported fashion brands. If we rate the growth of each of these companies from a future prospective, however, we will find that their growth has been stagnant. This situation puts our region far behind the rest of the world. If adaptability is accepted and deployed, however, and if professional consultants with proven records begin to assist owners, they will begin to see their companies flourish. Professionalization of company leadership is thus a vitally important step in building a company—there must be strong insight into all needs in order to ensure proper growth for any company.

Now that we have identified the overall reality and the drawbacks of the market in the region, in addition to some vision of our potential, let's look at some of the common mistakes we tend to make. These mistakes will be accompanied by a discussion of some general corrections that need to be made in order for eccentric marketing to be applied effectively.

Chapter 4:
Mistakes and Solutions

Marketing is a process by which a product or service is designed, created and continually refined to fulfill the target audience's needs. In today's market, it is a sense of creativity and innovation regarding a given concept which allows marketing to be completely successful. One compelling consideration in our context is how to address the problem of brand and product redundancy. Business owners must realize that in the Middle East and globally, there are a great many redundant competing product brands. The question, therefore, becomes which of these will survive and thrive?

The answer is simple. The first brand that dominates the consciousness of the consumer will be the survivor. Dominating a consumer category (i.e., a specific age group or a perceived life-style) occurs based on the success of marketing and branding. Thus, the importance of marketing in any given organization must not be taken lightly. Marketing is the heart, the engine, the essential essence if you will, that promotes the organization and its products and services. Marketing, as well as brand attention and innovation, is simply indispensible. In our region, however, there are many obstacles that an ascendancy of marketing faces, and therefore our brands are currently failing to fully achieve their potential. This section describes the five most common operating procedures, beliefs and practices (or lack of these things) from which our region suffers. After each section, a solution, including a variety of essential marketing principles, is described.

Mistake #1: Our CEOs Operate "My Way or No Way"

"My Way or No Way" is the basic attitude that CEOs in our region hold toward the role of marketing. Owning and running a business and making sales, unfortunately, are pursuits which tend to be held in service and intimately bound up with what in reality is often the company's true, if unwritten, primary goal: satisfying the owner's ego. If there is to be ego in marketing, it is preferable that the ego be infused with knowledge, rather than just a dictum which proceeds from the assumption of the intrinsic rightness of "My Way." That mode of thinking is a killer for the potential success of any brand.

It is true that as CEO one must oversee the total business process. But in the Middle Eastern context, the hard-headed CEO may decide within the scant space of a second to change the course of a company for what may be very personal, even pathological, reasons, rather than for the sake of the business. As the owner and the person responsible for the brand's life cycle, the hard-headed CEO will face decline much sooner because of the prominence of decisions based on impulsive behavior. What I am saying here is that the very embrace of a "My Way" approach clouds thinking and judgment, precisely because it blocks out other points of view, which is to say, it tends to block out reality.

The sad fact is that many of our region's CEOs decide the fate of their brands based almost solely on personal preferences. The owner's ego and impulsive behavior make it more important to him to appear to be high on the totem pole than to nurture the total life of the organization and its objectives.

Another fact of most Arab companies in the region is that they are solely owned by a single family. We find that the upper management of these companies generally consists of members of the controlling family, whether those family members have any experience in the business at hand or not. The decisions made by company management will thus tend to reflect what the family says, or how the family wishes to present itself, rather than the actual facts of the market, and this concern for satisfying the needs of the family tends to supersede any contemplation of the best moves the company might otherwise make based on increasing sales, securing financing, or establishing a brand.

I have seen first-hand how some brands have completely vanished from the market, due to a hard-headed, egotistical CEO who decides that he is right and that the true process of marketing is wrong. They never try to understand their responsibility to the brand until reality strikes, if even then. Let's look at how we might be able to change this baleful situation.

Solution #1: Clearly Define Responsibilities

No matter how qualified or unqualified, it is the business owner who ultimately decides the fate of his firm. The egotistical owner who decides to be CEO must realize what it really takes to be a CEO, for the sake of his company and for the Arab region—for all who want to go to the global market with their brands. When the owner of a business also acts as its CEO, all too often he assigns himself the title without understating the explicit details of his job description. Therefore, a fundamental first step is to understand what precisely a CEO is supposed to do for his or her company to thrive.

First, especially when a CEO has trouble reading between the lines regarding the opportunities that the company's brands represent, he should clearly define the responsibilities in the firm and hire experts to fulfill the necessary roles. The owner must above all be willing to hire and listen to professionals.

The two titles—owner and CEO—have distinguishably different goals. The owner's goal is to set up the company and state the major goals of his organization. If the owner is financially capable, but not well-equipped with the managerial skills necessary to efficiently run the organization, he should hire a properly qualified, credentialed proxy to operate his organization—a CEO. Doing so will ensure the long-term survival of the company, of the owner himself, and ultimately of our nation.

A CEO has the full-time job of overseeing the overall operation of the organization. He has the commitment and the responsibility to provide for the company's success on behalf of the shareholders, and reports directly to the Board. The CEO's job from the start-up of the company is to envision the company's overall planning and strategy, to delegate authority and duties appropriately, to oversee the company's operations, and to ensure that the company operates efficiently in all these matters. He is also responsible for approving the company's operational procedures, policies and standards and conducting direct company planning, often via formation of a policy-making committee, and much more. The qualified CEO will ensure that the company is achieving its goals and receiving appropriate rewards. He can establish a proper management strategy to penetrate more assets and raise the total equity of the firm. He will hire upper-level managers as needed to assist him in implementing the organization's goals. He will delegate accordingly and see that the all the designated tasks are achieved.

Given the monumental duties of a functioning CEO, the owner must strive to be modest and manage by supplying overarching objectives in order for the company's brands to reach the global marketplace. Hard-headed owner/CEOs often don't realize the risk to the brand's value until trouble hits. To fix problems at this point is not an easy process, and it is expensive. Instead, the decisions concerning a brand's life should be carefully analyzed, planned and organized in a deliberate way. This process should not be based on assumptions and personal preferences, but on facts and market reality, in order for the brand to achieve its objectives. The owner must put his ego aside for the benefit of his products and his company. There are many qualified CEOs in our region who can assist in setting up a proper structure for a company's organization. There are many qualified businesspeople who can ensure that the organization stays intact and self-sufficient.

A few courageous business owners have taken this major step and the move has paid them back abundantly. Their organizations are able and willing to move forward with their strategy to serve more countries within and outside the region. One example would be Bison, the locally-produced energy drink here in Saudi

Arabia. This brand serves the entire region while working its way toward serving other regions, including Africa, according to a representative of the company.

Unfortunately, that business decision to hire in competent help is seldom decided based on business reasons in our region. Instead, such a decision tends to be all about levels of self-esteem. If at one point the firm is doing quite well and is working hard to expand its efforts into new geographical areas, the owner might decide to fire the CEO to save money in order to insure that the company can continue to pay his high salary. In the worst-case scenario, the owner will decide to install himself or his son as the CEO, believing that doing so will push things forward, or perhaps in order to keep that CEO salary in the family. The question that such a dubious decision raises is: What will the end result be?

Owners in our region seem never to take responsibility for their companies; they are all too frequently intent on working to preserve the credibility of their belief that they are always right and the rest of the world is wrong, wherever the two differ. But the owner's responsibility should not be to their families only—even in the absence of shareholders in the company, their responsibility should be to our nation as a whole. Our nation expects business owners to flourish, to support the total mechanism of the local economy, including exports and national branding. The differences in risks involved with being an owner versus being a CEO are tremendous. A qualified CEO has the experience to run the organization and reduce its risks. A qualified CEO reduces the chance of the company shutting down or going out of business. If things are not established clearly, then the company's maturity will never progress, and it will probably decline. I am sorry to say that a company operating under those conditions will operate either only as a small business or it will finally fade from existence.

For a business owner to hire a competent CEO to run the business is a simple idea, but it should be a well-reasoned decision. The question is: are we working for own personal satisfaction, or do we have a responsibility to the Middle East region? Do we understand that we must help our nation compete properly in this era of globalization? Are we thinking globally, or merely flexing our muscles to satisfy our self-esteem? If the owners of the businesses in our region understand the role of a CEO, then we can expect our businesses to flourish strategically around the globe.

Mistake #2: Operating by Assumption

Many of our brands are built on personal assumptions on the part of people who possess only the lowest degree of basic marketing knowledge. Marketing, however, cannot rest on assumptions, only on facts and innovative ideas. So what, exactly, is "assumption marketing?" Assumption marketing occurs when a business owner sits with his relatives and friends and decides to buy, import or even produce products merely *assuming* those products will sell in the market based on the personal feelings of whoever is assembled at the time. The owner then decides to produce the product or even import it without understanding his target audience or the segment of the market to which he intends to address his product. The initial business decision—to decide to produce the product—was based on assumptions, not on market need. His total marketing plan is one big assumption as to who his direct target audience actually might be.

Many small-scale and larger-scale operations have been guilty of pursuing the assumption-based approach, to the extent that assumption-making has become a process of marketing in our region. This is a very negative trend that has been a large part of our falling behind the rest of the world. For example, a larger-scale operation that launched its brand thirty years ago may have seen its market share dwindle to a few percentage points simply because its leaders have disregarded the importance of marketing. Despite seeing the small losses over time, these leaders figured that they were doing "well enough" that they should just let things continue "as is." What the CEO does, however, is blame the marketing department, even though he hasn't relied on it for guidance. By contrast, other CEOs may hire unqualified employees to manage sensitive departments such as marketing. These two problems—blaming a marketing department that has no power and hiring unqualified employees—can turn into a vicious cycle. The real question is this, however: Is basing a business plan on an assumption risky to any new or existing brand or idea? The answer is an obvious and resounding "Yes!" Ask any reputable financial consultant and see what he or she has to say.

Solution #2: Operate with Intent, Hire the Right People

The idea of operating with intent and hiring the right people returns us to our discussion of the CEO. First, the qualified CEO will hire those who best fit the firm and its objectives. Establishing the proper qualifications for each position is the CEO's most important responsibility in the overall process of his Human Resources department. The qualified CEO will hire the best people who have the best qualifications to fulfill the job responsibilities required. For example, as with the unqualified owner, the unqualified CEO will hire based on favoritism and assumptions.

Operating with intent means planning and implementing marketing strategies. Many of us in this part of the world pay far less attention to marketing than we should. We'd rather focus on the tangible aspects of selling products and services, as when we estimate that the total equity of the product lies exclusively in its good taste or its functionality. We also wrongly assume that all it takes to beat our competition is to make sure our product is much better. Really, in all decisions related to our brands, we should operate with *intent*—using the principles described later in this book—and not on assumptions.

It is my contention that brand marketing should be left to marketers and not to the CEO of the organization. The marketer, to be successful, will be well-equipped with appropriate knowledge and experience. If the business owner does not understand what marketing is, he should hire a firm that will structure the organization properly and deploy the most qualified employees for each job in the structure, especially if the position to be filled is that of CEO.

To avoid following the assumption marketing paradigm at the inception of the company, it is important that the company hire the right players and clearly define long- and short-term objectives. These objectives must be well aligned with the overall company brand objective. We need not look very far to see some successful companies that operate in this fashion. For example, many local Dubai brands in the United Arab Emirates have broken into the global market. Think of Emirates Air Lines, for example. They were a small market player a decade ago, and today they are one of the fastest growing brands in the industry. Why? Ask the CEO. He had a vision and made sure that the brand he created would fulfill its promise. Further, the city of Dubai is a world-wide brand destination for real estate, shopping and lifestyle. On the business-to-business side, the strongest Arab brands are SABIC and the Port of Dubai.

Were these brands built on assumptions? Not at all! The CEOs of these brands know exactly what their short-term and long-term plans are for their brands. We must avoid the dangerous risks of operating our businesses based on assumptions. Those responsible for ensuring this happens are the business owners or the brand owners, more so than the members of the organization. Still, both groups—top management and employees—need to work together toward common, well-established goals.

A brief note here: I glimpse a potential for a perhaps well-intentioned owner or CEO to give the name of market research to some rather informal and improvised arrangements of family and friends. In other words, it may not be as simple as it seems to forsake the assumption approach if one is not aware that one's process is based on assumption. Coffee with friends is not focus grouping. If a business owner is in doubt about whether his methods rely on assumption, again, he would do well to confer with a qualified academic or professional.

Mistake #3: We Don't Listen and Adapt

My argument is not completely concerned with the actions of the business owner, as may have been implied up to this point. Rather, it is about long-term strategies for our brands to flourish globally. The core of the problem, however, is that the owner of the private business in our context frequently decides to do his own thing, no matter what the risk level is—*he doesn't listen.*

I often sit and wonder why we seem to find it so difficult to open our ears and minds and listen to those who know a lot more than we do about various subjects one way or the other. I consider the biggest risk for the Arab world to be that we will never enjoy a global competitive edge if we don't improve how we think about our business operations. There are times when running a privately-owned, conglomerated organization that we must consider asking those who are *business builders* to assist us. Otherwise, it will be someday be too late for us to do so, and we will end up on the consumer and importer end of business relations forever.

Reliance on good research and solid information is actually an important kind of listening. Many owners and CEOs can't seem to do even this kind of listening. They approach marketing from a theoretical perspective, under which mere opinions are put forth and millions of dollars are invested in the product or service based on those opinions—without ever doing the research in terms of surveys, focus groups, or field work necessary to clearly identify who the real audience for a product actually is. Money does not grow on trees, and products will never move off the supermarket shelves unless they are clearly understood by the target audience and they suit that audience's needs and behaviors. Business owners must be aware of the risk that is involved in disregarding market research! We would do well in this regard to take notice of the examples of those who built up proper marketing foundations. The end result is that their brands maintain a healthy cash flow.

Solution #3: Listen to Those Who Know and Begin to Change

It is imperative that we change our thinking in order to flourish and become producers of mass brands. We must break from tradition and adopt proper organizational structures adaptable to a global economy. We must employ those who know how to assist us in making this shift. Doing so is the only way we will flourish as firms and brands.

We must recognize that the region's trading methodology has changed from the way our forefathers operated; therefore, we must adapt to those changes as necessary to pursue our present aims. This willingness to adapt must start with the owner of the operation. This very simple paradigm shift can transport us to higher levels and entrench us in the global market, not just with a few brands, but with more and more. If we are able to make this shift, which is after all a simple shift in our manner of thinking, then one day I have no doubt that we as a region we will be efficiently branded and a recognized global player.

To become a global player, we must listen to those who through expertise and accomplishment have earned a place as leaders. Leaders set examples, and we must follow those examples in order to proceed toward a brighter tomorrow. For example, the Commerce Ministries should provide models for business owners to obtain the required licenses. Most businesses are currently applying for a general trade license, which accounts for basically about 85 percent of our market today. Retail owners gear themselves to import foreign goods, because local consumers trust the quality of imported goods. If we produce and enforce proper strategies and plans, however, we will also build consumer confidence in our own products. This effect applies to many elements of a business. If you have a general trading company, the most important factor is a proper marketing plan. Business owners must educate themselves on all aspects of marketing, such as creating their own brands and setting up a proper marketing department in order to achieve overall goals.

This situation begs the question: why should we stick merely to trade? Things are changing; for the future to be bright, we must do things right today. For example, every decade we face new generations of potential buyers of our consumer brands. If we don't address these new generations and their preferences, we will likely experience a generational decline in business. Future consumers will not act or behave as our forefathers did, or even as we do. They will have their own needs as consumers and they have no reason to allow old ways of trading to be forced upon them. Their alternative will be to move on to well-represented, imported brands, because the makers of these have taken the trouble to cater their brands and their products to the consumers' needs and behaviors, rather than buying goods produced within the Arab world.

The key, therefore, is adaptability. The new generation is adapting the means by which their fathers conducted the trade business such that these means have become a continuous cycle through the generations. This continuity seems reassuring. It should actually be frightening. One day we will be cornered and find that our resources have not been used properly to reach our product's consumers.

Mistake #4: We use our money muscle the wrong way

Does money wield muscle? Of course. And one need not look far to name brands which have turned cash flow into making their business grow and thrive by wielding their money muscle to build the brand and the business—Emirates Airlines, Mercedes, Microsoft and Starbucks are good examples of brands that are well-recognized worldwide and generate major cash flow. In our own market reality, however, we too frequently consider it a waste of money to create a brand using the proper tools. We may pour all of our concentration and money into production and quality of taste, for example. But the fact is that our consumers are under no obligation to think the same way as the owner of the company. The owner invests millions of dollars on production and manpower, yet the marketing department consists not of marketers, but of salespeople who join the force of *distribution*—"push and shove" is what I call the way they do marketing.

According to the owner, the plant should perform miracles in term of sales. When owners are asked, "Why you don't consider a proper marketing plan or set up a proper marketing department, fully equipped with manpower and a proper budget?" Their answer is inevitably: "Why spend when I can save?" But how is the owner saving money when his market share is declining? In reality, he is losing money, and in the near future he will be faced with the prospect of selling the company as depreciated equipment.

The other dilemma is that business owners expect simple advertising to bring about the desired end result without having applied proper marketing logistics and a clear marketing plan—or even without constructing a proper brand-building strategy, including positioning and personification.

Here is the truth about advertising: your advertising spending can be enormous and never translate into actual sales. Advertising has become a mindless trend and a thought-free option. Moreover, the losses a company incurs by dumping millions into an advertising budget are not merely financial. Intense publicity of an ill-conceived brand can amount to advertising your company's incompetence. In that case, the more you spend on advertising, the worse it is for your business in the long run. The damage in that case can be permanent, or fatal. Once a brand is registered in the consumer's mind as a poorly experienced brand, it is hard to change that perception, such that to rebuild a positive brand image in such a case would almost invariably be prohibitively expensive.

Other companies spend millions on the brand communication stage without first having established a proper marketing platform. Whenever you launch a mass consumer product, the plan given to the marketing department is to reach everyone through communication and make sure the product is well-distributed. What happens if these relatively new brands are competing against strong brands that are already dominant in the market? These generic marketers still rely solely on the generic marketing mix and rely exclusively on communication to try to reach ultimate brand results. This approach is completely wrong. If positioning, market segmentation and strategy are not deployed along with a well-planned marketing mix, then you will have problems seeing the brand become a recognizable part of people's lives.

I have seen case after case of this failure. For instance, I have seen many television advertisements for a new brand in the market. Often, there would be nothing different about the "new" brand, except a different name, a different color logo and a lame slogan with no clear-cut positioning. What happens next is that the brand will decline gradually until it dies a natural death. The waste generated is not associated with the product alone; it is everything else that was built along with the product.

Solution #4: Use Your Money Wisely

The solution to the mistake of using money in the wrong ways is simple: exert your money muscle during the formative months of a brand's introduction. Failure to do so is one of the primary reasons we are still in the early stages of understanding what marketing truly is in the Middle East. We have professional marketers in the region who are ready to assist any owner with his marketing and to help establish a marketing department. Doing so is crucial if the owner wishes to attain positive results for his firm. There are a few owners in the region who follow the proper method of marketing and use their money muscle to capitalize on the brand. For example, the real estate giant Emaar, Emirates Airlines and DP World are all brands based in Dubai. I give them credit for how far they have come in their market maturity, and I am pleased to have observed that their market penetration has grown geographically as a result of those efforts. These brands have great potential for widening their scope to new regions outside our own. Already, Emaar operates outside of the region, and Emirates Airlines, as we have discussed, has grown rapidly as well.

In addition to applying money muscle at the right place and at the right time, there are several ways to use the power of business money wisely, including outsourcing and wisely valuing brands.

Outsourcing is an excellent way for a business to use its money wisely. China has become a major production hub for both Middle East-branded products and non-branded daily use items. Many of the firms that plan to brand their products for a middle-class audience use China as a production hub. Usually these firms work in the apparel, household items and furniture industries, and outsourcing is beneficial simply in terms of cost efficiency.

I support outsourcing in cases where a firm plans to invest and capitalize on brands that can penetrate both within the region and outside the region. Efficiency is the key here. There are many advantages to looking elsewhere for cheaper labor that will produce products according to a firm's standards. The United States, for example, has been a key player in the past and present in outsourcing; many major American brands are produced in the Asia-Pacific region. Now, China has become a hub for the Middle East even more so than for the United States. This set of circumstances has emerged primarily to import restrictions and quotas applied by the U.S. on Chinese textiles and apparel.

Because the firms using China as a production hub have cut costs by outsourcing, they have the money to focus on building their brands. Perhaps the critical question is whether they know how to accomplish this task in the best manner possible. I believe that there are many brand-building specialists that can help these firms capitalize on their brands. But those experts will be able to be of service only if the owner of the brand has a thorough understanding of brand value.

At times you may have seen a foreign retail brand operating in your city and generating enormous traffic. At the same time, the firm's merchandise is made in China. The owner of the competing local brand asks himself, "Why is this happening? Why not my firm?" The difference is that the foreign retailer invested more in positioning its brands so that it could properly communicate with its target audience, even while outsourcing its merchandise to China or Taiwan. It is quite a simple concept—outsourcing for production is a great way to go, if it can save you money. Money saved on production can then be redirected to capitalize on marketing and branding in order to attain and maintain a strong consumer base.

The goal of U.S. firms in outsourcing is to capitalize on their brand assets, while overseeing cost control and quality assurance. This approach allows many of their brands to serve a global market. Most of these firms have marketing strategies for their brands designed to attract a certain target audience demographic from around the world. Are we in the Middle East heading in that direction? At present, I believe not. Too few Arab firms are thinking about, trying to understand, or applying the models for market penetration that have worked elsewhere. Some, however, have been successful in adopting new ways of thinking that have emerged based on global competition. The major question for these firms in our region related to outsourcing is: Are they capitalizing on their brands? Or are they still confused about the brand's value?

Many tend to believe that simply devising an attractive logo will do the job, rather than aligning the total brand with consumer needs, building its personality, and differentiating their brands from those of their competitors.

Mistake #5: Failure to Innovate.

Although we in the Arab world have a well-equipped society, many of our innovators must still travel abroad to fully realize their dreams. Marketers in our region are fully equipped to implement the total marketing process and create successful brands. The problem is not with the marketers—it is with the owners of the firms. A publicly-traded company does not have this problem in our region, but how many of those exist? Not many—the majority of firms are privately owned and most of those are small-scale. Growth comes when the brand is adequately competitive and well-built. Unfortunately, we lack the tendency to regard the brand as a source of income. And without the proper awareness of the brand, it is hard for the product to reach distributors.

Further, a recurring pattern has been for our firms to try to make recapitulation pass for innovation. Regional businesses move quickly to copy a success story; in a few months to a year following a successful brand, Six to seven other brands are trying to copy it. The funny thing is that most of the newcomers' board members will sit and discuss market share—is their market share growing, or are they spending enough on advertising to increase market share by 5%? How much money will you need to dump into advertising to gain a single point of market share? If you have to spend millions, how will you ever earn a return?

Obviously, how to increase the market share of a copycat product is not the right question to be asking. As I have already established, the marketing department in some of these companies is good for nothing. That's because their understanding of marketing is basically limited to appearing in every medium possible, whether or not that medium truly targets their core audience—or whether there's a viable brand to be marketed in the first place. They simply go for what they call "presence."

I suppose the belief in and reliance on advertising is natural. But I would encourage those relying on advertising to think of a brand like Starbucks. It is a mega-brand known worldwide. Do you see advertisements for it everywhere? Hardly! Yet you see Starbucks stores everywhere; in major cities, you can probably see the stores on every other block.

Unfortunately, we in the Middle East tend to take the world of marketing, creativity and innovation very lightly. We often consider a brand to be nothing more than a logo printed on a printing press. A brand is much, much more than that. And, gentlemen, owners, if you are reading this book, you must admit you have realized that the overall marketing process in today's world is quite different from how it was during the days when your forefathers were trading. Copying other models does not assist us in breaking into the global market, and it is another way to tag a company with a bad reputation before it has scarcely gotten off the ground.

On one occasion—and I was a personal witness to this—an investor asked me to replicate something he had seen working in the local market. The object of his interest was the dominant brand in the market, and I immediately decided there was no way I would put my neck and my reputation on the line to do as he asked. The brand he liked had been the first in its category, and was known for its strong selling propositions. It had been well-registered with its target audience—enough so that when you mentioned the brand name, the average consumer could tell you what the product line entailed. I sat in my house and thought about my conversation with this investor. What had he been thinking? Why didn't he want to become a dominant brand leader in another area, rather than trying to break into a market where he knew that he didn't have a chance?

Solution #5: Keep our innovators home!

Innovation is what will help us advance our brands. When we think of building brands, we very frequently invite people from overseas firms to assist us. They bring with them their own innovations. The question is: When will we be innovators ourselves? When will an innovation be 100% our own? When will we differentiate and succeed in creating something that the whole world needs?

I ask myself these questions almost every day. What we have to do is to create what is needed. We have an opportunity—a huge opportunity—to become a global player. We should strive to keep our innovators at home! We should do what we must to give them the chance to excel. If we do, our region will begin to see the difference. One day we will have locally-created brands that will serve the global market. We can create brands that will bowl the world over in a wide variety of industries. We need to attain results.

So what strategies should one implement to address a target audience and fulfill their needs?

It is all about market planning and the level of risk business people are willing to take. Most investors are risk-takers, but they would do well to have proper insight into the market before taking even a minimal risk. As mentioned, a "good" risk is supposed by many business leaders to be one that copies a success. That is the most risk many are willing to take in our region, and, really, it is not even minimal. Our region is not risk-oriented when it comes to new ideas. Many won't even try to create a new category; they'd rather work with what exists. This aversion to risk is why we are limited to only a few industries. For example, if you come up with a new way to sell cars, then that might be a great business. But a few years later you may see a million other car dealers and agents popping up around the region. The same applies for other products.

And unfortunately it is all too often only when things go wrong that experts are called in to clean up the mess. As a marketer, however, I can tell you that it is very hard to resurrect a dead brand. The better approach would be to let it die and start anew, primarily because a dead brand means that the consumer has already had a bad experience and is not likely to give the brand another try. Ultimately, however, the next steps have always been the owner's call. He is the one, and the only one, who decides the fate of the brand. With this being the case, many owners are asking: "Why are we not penetrating the global market? Why are we not competitive with our foreign counterparts?" These questions can be answered only by the owner of the brand, who is, at the same time, the CEO—whether you like it or not. Movements are very forceful in the market; once it is decided, things move until brands are dead. This trend will continue to occur until you ask the owner to step aside, earn the money and let those who are professionals do their job. If these changes are not made today, while we are ready for them, then we can forget about our future and the future of our generations to come.

Business owners and entrepreneurs must start being innovative by realizing that things change every day; consumers change, and new generations are born to replace former generations. How do we carry on? I would plainly say that we must focus, innovate and be trendsetters. Today's brand mechanisms involve a vigorous psychoanalysis of consumer behavior and changes, but all these pursuits revolve around two main fundamentals: consumers' visual perception and their emotional bond to the brand. Innovation and creativity are the cornerstones of marketing, so keep reading!

Business leaders need to visit their mission and vision statements every now and then, to bring them closer to evolving understandings of market reality. In tackling all these problems and their solutions, business leaders may find that the market reality may go against the reality they would wish. They would tend to be very reluctant to accept mistakes and problems and to step down from their corporate positions, until they pass away or age out, because of the threat doing so would pose to their self-esteem. Such reluctance has undermined the collective responsibility of Arab nations as they seek to find ways to have their product brands appear on the international platform. CEOs have the job of delivering, leading their organizations to produce, and the ability to do so depends on their ability to foresee the unification of identity and action of the company internally and to pursue its greatest penetration externally.

Chapter 5:
Marketing 101—A Middle East Marketing How-To

As has been observed in preceding chapters in discussing mistakes and opportunities, the importance of marketing in 100% locally-owned firms in our region of the Arab world is still disregarded. Having a view of the mistakes we make and the tendencies which give rise to those mistakes, as well as a view of a range of general solutions to these issues, this chapter will establish a foundation for eccentric marketing.

The Four Ps

What we know as Marketing 101, or the basic principles of marketing, begin with the famous Four Ps—Product, Place, Price and Promotion—which Neil Borden introduced as "the marketing mix" during his presidential address to the American Marketing Association in 1953. The four P's are the basic ingredients of marketing. Combined, these elements work together to implement marketing strategies. The four Ps are:

1. **Product:** the object or service you would like to introduce to your target audience.

2. **Place**: the location of your business or the location where you want your product or service to be distributed or placed.
3. **Price**: what you wish your customer to pay for your product, which depends on competition, brand value and your target customer's income.
4. **Promotion**: the communication tools you use between the product and consumer, which include advertising, word of mouth and point of sale.

These are only the most basic principles of marketing, and many of us have encountered them in our university years. They are important—indispensible, even—but it is my contention that if we base everything on a simple view of the market mix as an operating factor of marketing within our organization, we have a major problem. For the special purposes and distinct needs of our region, I suggest some adjustments to the Four Ps as they are normally taught in school.

In short, creativity and innovation must be added to this basic foundation in order to implement eccentric marketing. Too many regional firms stop at the basic marketing mix and do not infuse their marketing with creativity and innovation. For example, calculate the monetary value of sixty salesmen fighting their way through a tight market or category. Things become so cluttered that the cost of the marketing department outweighs the total income generated. In this environment, the lack of innovation and creativity holds the brand back. The four P's are not enough.

Consumers expect changes and trends, especially younger consumers. Marketing applications are continuously evolving as more marketers act innovatively to attain end results for their brands. New strategies—those that include innovation and creativity—are ways in which you can break loose from your competition. Such new thinking should embrace your total communication strategy to introduce your brand to the market.

Thus, marketing mix plus innovation equals brand success. Let's look in general at the four P's and how businesses in the

Middle East can add creativity and innovation to each piece of the marketing mix.

Allow me to address business owners directly, and start by providing some specific examples of **product categories**. The simple definition of a product category is that it is comprised of two or more products that embody the same reasons and purposes. The dairy product, milk, is a category, carbonated drinks are a category, and local and imported produce is also a category. Once you have identified your category, ask yourself some questions:

1. How cluttered is your consumer product category?
2. Are consumers given many choices in your category?
3. What is the market share of the companies who are massively penetrating this category?
4. What is the total target population within each category? Can you observe the total population?
5. What if the category serves only about 8% of the total population? Is that substantial enough to support several brands from different companies?

Each category can include the original concept or the stamp of the brand's creator, but what we witness in our region is an overcrowding of brands within the same category. They are all targeting the same audience, very frequently with the same key word as a slogan. The perfect example of this in our region is the fresh milk category originated by Almarai. This company actually "owns" the fresh milk category and identifies its product as fresh milk. Others have joined the category over time, and today we have five to six brands in the same category—but they cannot differentiate themselves. The category has become tight and the consumer will likely set his mind on the first or second brand that was launched.

Once you've answered these questions about your product, it is more important to think about which **segment** of the consumer market you are targeting. A category can contain many segments of a target audience. For example, some companies may target a demographic of women in their thirties or forties. Others could target the demographic of pregnant women. Each segment is homogeneous in their behavior and needs, so they might respond quickly to a given marketing strategy.

How far can a category expand to meet the needs of a particular segment? Not far. A category is like a nation—if the nation cannot meet certain needs of the population, then that nation starts introducing things like home planning awareness according to that country's economic scale. Like nations, everything has a limit and a boundary. You can stretch a brand, but if you wish to stretch the category, you'll need to explore new geographical markets. To penetrate the same market means to be aware of its limit. We have to accept that our consumers are well aware of their needs and we must thus consider their view of those needs in order to realize there are limits. We must therefore consider segmentation, because it gives us a wider scope for differentiation and reaching a wider audience.

Your product category and consumer segment will determine your **place** and **promotion** strategies. It doesn't help to place your product in a discount store if you are creating a luxury brand for high-income consumers. Likewise, it doesn't help to gain endorsements from someone in the juice industry if your product is a chauffeur service. These examples may seem overly simplistic, but you'd be amazed at how often business owners ignore these considerations. As I have mentioned, my opinion is that **pricing** should not necessarily be part of your marketing mix. It can become a factor in segmenting products, however, as you define your brand profile and the social class for which your brand is intended. If you have a problem seeing your produce in a particular category, then why not create a category and build on it?

The Middle East is quite limited in terms of industrial offerings—most markets are composed of up to 85% consumer-goods retailers. That's why we have more retail banking, and the numbers of those retail banks are growing according to need. This trend makes a lot of sense. It is a given that we have high spending per capita, but consumers like to explore and experience new trends. The newer generations are different from the older generation. What my dad likes is not the same as what I like, and what my son likes is not the same either.

So how do we go beyond the generic Four Ps and marketing mix to extend the reach of our brands?

The Emerging markets

Brazil, Russia, India, and China are frequently referred to collectively as the BRIC countries. Together they represent one of the major emerging markets, especially for China, the hub of world mass production and for meeting the demands of each country. My subject is not to discuss the emerging markets so much, given the fact that most business owners, and most Middle Eastern countries, are not from the advanced emerging markets but from secondary countries, such as Egypt, Morocco, Jordan, Qatar, Kuwait and the UAE. In some cases only Egypt and Morocco are considered as being from secondary emerging markets. With such an opportunity most of the CEOs from these countries could have turned the tables around and capitalized on any of a variety of factors in order to reach their firms' expectations.

As important as this line of inquiry is, however, I wouldn't hold myself out as an economist and sit here and try to analyze the emerging markets as if I knew the entire process. What really interests me is that these countries have exerted the effort to climb the ladder by industrializing themselves to attract both local and foreign investors. Some countries have over-forecast their expectations and applied some extremely rigged-together investment policies, and the result in some cases was turmoil and failure. At times the habit of proceeding from assumptions rather than knowledge can drive expectations in the wrong directions, and some countries have done just that. Then, too, many ran pell-mell in the PR direction to boost their achievements even when the results of doing so continued to be minimal.

What do most of our CEOs understand about the emerging markets? Are they heading in a direction to capitalize on growth? What are the long-term and short-term plans for these local firms in terms of developing a relationship with the emerging markets? Usually these emerging markets are branded for perhaps one thing that was negative, and for a few positives, but again our CEOs are not well positioned to articulate and evoke potential, but are driven by perceptions. For example, in social gatherings populated by CEOs, "Be in Paris," "Open in London" and "Open in New York," are some phrases you often hear thrown around at coffee table meetings. The emerging markets, such as Russia, Brazil and China, are less appealing to them simply because such nations don't do the work these CEOs truly require of business endeavors: providing a cure for their low self esteem.

I wish these business owners and CEOs would wake up and realize the potential for their brands across the world and stop living the European dreams that will eventually vanish because they will be obsolete. Consider this: Why did the G7 change to the G20? In whose interest is that? I would say it is in the interest of the initial G7 countries to balance the current equation. This is especially so considering that China's interest in the US is a two-way road, given that China is buying a great many US Bonds and the US is one of the largest importers of Chinese readymade and non-readymade goods.

Chapter 6:
Corporate Strategy

If we were to simply define what corporate strategy is in a few words, we would find that job as simple as reciting the business dictionary definition:

An approach to the future that involves (1) examination of the current and anticipated factors associated with customers and competitors (external environment) and the firm itself (internal environment), (2) envisioning a new or more effective role for the firm in a creative manner, and (3) aligning policies, practices and resources to realize that vision.

This process as defined above can only produce discomfort for most business owners in our region. Such development would be a very complex issue, considering that implementation and control processes are what see the details of the corporate strategy through. As long as formulation of a viable corporate strategy is completely out of the picture for most of the organizations in the region, there is ample room for doubt that a proper marketing strategy could be properly processed, and still more room for skepticism that a strategy could be executed.

Do most Middle Eastern companies apply a corporate strategy system? Do they understand what such a strategy means, the benefits they might expect to derive from it, and what such a strategy would require of them? It has been my experience that most people in positions of company leadership in our region do not know. I have witnessed this knowledge gap repeatedly through our marketing consultancies for several firms which are reputable by name but whose reputation exceeds their performance. In such instances again, the internal forces are usually shaky when we come with the big questions we need to ask in order for us to develop a strategy. Do you have a corporate strategy? May I see your external strategy? In both cases the answer is almost always "no." But again most people in positions of company leadership assume they do have and know it, when the fact is that they don't know. Some even pass over their corporate profile and simply say, "That's all we have." For God's sake, how?

Again the ego-driven process has caused these business leaders to neglect the most essential part of their business fundamentals. So the question becomes, how do most of these leaders develop the corporate mission and vision without a simple SWOT analysis, and how do they state their mission and vision statements on all their company imprints without assessing the strategy that will take them there? The second part of the puzzle is, how do companies run their brands as business lines without unified strategic objectives that will eventually support the total unified corporate initiative? Such an initiative could be a strong theory that those admirable CEOs would find it difficult to ignore, but again they don't even believe in theories, being, by and large, only great replicators of what exists, the trend leaders of me-too brands, in the trend we discussed above of business leaders copying a successful existing brand.

So if people are still only copying brands then why would they even need a corporate strategy? Why have all those words on paper and no one to implement them? We don't have credentialed or qualified employees. Our human resources departments seek instead to hire affordable low-price employees. This scenario is quite common among the CEOs and business owners who are running many of the midsized companies.

What would I advise? I have tried to advise many of these CEOs and owners, but they are still insisting on living in their own rarified realm, while time is hastening away in front of their noses. One of the other things I have also realized with regard to the change from being traders to being business people is that it is not an easy process for many people to undertake. The trader's mindset drives the market to be heavy in retail concerns, such that many of the Middle East markets are composed mainly of retailers. This situation explains why research has shown that more retail banking is needed, although most of the countries in the region are now swamped by locally and internationally branded banks. So in terms of moving from being traders to being businessmen capable of organizing a modern business, how long would it take for such a change to take place?

The current trends suggest that companies are gearing towards setting up organized businesses in the trade businesses that their forefathers used to run. But still the question remains as to how deeply the trader's mentality of imports and exports is entrenched in the hearts of the business culture. Or perhaps we might better refer to their area of concern as "import and sell to local retailers." It seems safe to say that for the majority of business owners, this approach won't fade out for generations to come, such that it will be perhaps two more decades until it begins to fade in earnest. So where do our organizations stand in the middle of all this trading mess? It is safe to say that they are finding themselves in the middle of a deep haze. Funnily enough, I believe that the world of corporate strategy is still new and yet to be explored by many trading firms that we would wish to be competitive in this world of organized business.

All that being said, directors, CMOs and marketing consultants alike need the external impetus of the corporate strategy in order to deliver an effectively oriented strategy. With this in mind I would heartily recommend and advise every company from mid-size to large to consider this advice before it is too late. Do you ever wonder why so many firms suffer during their initial stages? Do you ever wonder why these firms never had a sense of direction and frequently engaged in multiple businesses, often poorly or half-heartedly? These things happened because these firms never defined their strategic objectives or corporate initiatives.

The decision of a CEO or business owner to seriously consider adopting a corporate strategy could have redemptive power for many companies both in terms of short term and long term strategies. Adopting a corporate strategy could help business owners and CEOs control the process of moving their organization toward a single strategic goal or objective.

Chapter 7:
Marketing vs. Advertising

Marketing is the process by which companies create customer interest in goods or services. It generates the strategy that underlies sales techniques, business communication, and business development. It is an integrated process through which companies build strong customer relations and creates value for their customers and for themselves. (Wikipedia)

Marketing Moves On: We Stand Still

The understanding of marketing among CEOs and businesses in the Middle East: anything that has to do with sales and advertising. This is a conception which takes away the end value of what marketing actually is. CEOs may generally be agreeable to the idea that marketing is responsible for sales, but in reality marketing should also be responsible for anything that is external to the company and that is directly associated or linked to the consumer. So how much of that do CEOs and business owners in the Arab world understand?

There's a great deal to marketing beyond an understanding of the basic principles articulated in the 4 Ps, obviously. For one thing, there are no longer just four Ps in the marketing mix. In addition to the 4 Ps listed above—Product, Place, Price, and Promotion—marketing theorists have recently embraced three more concepts as being fundamental: People, Process, and Physical Evidence. Each of these 7 Ps of marketing, which taken together may still be known as the marketing mix, has a direct effect on the consumer's decision to buy a service or product. If you consider these principles as a start in marketing you're moving in the right direction, but even then, you may still be residing in the basic principles of marketing and its foundations.

The story of marketing goes back quite far, hearkening back to the simple strategies used in the industrial era in America in the early 30's. But every decade after the beginning of the story up until today the situation has been changing in response to a changing society and its ever new needs and demands. Always, it seems the models showing what marketing is must change their nature to suit the business circumstances of each successive era and to respond to the shift of industry from manufacturing to service and to online business, which is taking off rapidly, especially with the growth of social media.

When I attended the University of Maine at Machias my first course in marketing was Principles of Marketing, Marketing 101, and it was no longer ago than that when, according to the American Marketing Association, there were only 4 Ps of marketing. Today there are seven, and that's just the change in the past twenty years. Will we perhaps see more Ps in the future? Likely so. Given the changing demands and the ongoing growth and the changing nature of the world economy I believe we will soon be up to 11 Ps.

However that may be, once the principles of marketing are in place, and once we have acknowledged that these principles must be continually reviewed and updated, then there opens up a world of a great variety of strategies for aligning a company with those principles. These strategies, between their function and their attributes, should be the cornerstone of a company's brand, and should take priority in the early stages of product development, far prior to the company leadership embracing the empty promises of advertising.

But for our purposes, given all this rapid innovation, the important question is, how many of the CEOs in the Middle East region are ready to engage in modern marketing? This book is not about strategies. It is about the CEOs and the state of marketing in the Middle East, and about how business leaders have fallen into the trap of advertising being the cultural trend for spreading a company's message to customers' minds instead of marketing. Thus, it will be useful to bring out more of the reality of what passes for marketing in the Middle East.

Advertising: The Middle Eastern Businessman's Dead-End Path

Marketing in the Middle East is sales and advertising, and nothing of what I have talked about above. It is quite sad to me to contemplate how matters ever reached this point, and have come to a state in which millions of dollars are spent while brands never receive either their desired sales results or positive consumer recognition.

As long as the advertising industry is the de facto ruler of the marketing functionality of any firm then we are all doomed before doomsday. I offer this argument from experience with all the Middle Eastern brands I have worked on and with many brands I didn't. I am talking about CEOs and business owners who are half asleep in case after case, and not trying to put the simplest efforts into understand what marketing is. I could supply examples of such cases, but again my examples could be very hurtful to the advertising industry and many of the CEOs I have dealt with.

I must also say that there are CEOs whom I have met who have shown a willingness to drive the needed change and do themselves and their companies a great favor by avoiding spending on advertising and implementing real marketing courses of action. I only hope that more of such a willingness to change will be in evidence soon, and that the industry will be able to breathe and grow as proper marketing function rules out over a cluttered advertising industry which attains no results.

Advertising agencies run for the buck. They are like a drug store that sells all kinds of prescriptions over the counter. Some firms are managed by people who are so inexperienced, it starts to seem as though an agency license must be the easiest license there is to obtain. Funnily enough, through some of my research I have found that there are some countries within the region which have issued over *300,000* advertising licenses. So imagine: if you count most of the countries within the MENA region (Middle East North Africa) I'll bet that even the US itself does not boast of this many holders of agency licenses. What in the world are we thinking? We have many great minds and several great brands, and no shortage of great ideas. Why are we letting these hopeless CEOs manage all these assets simply because they are related to us in one way or another? Let's walk toward the future using proper guidelines and see if we can manage to build a sound grounding and a proper understanding of what marketing is.

Chapter 8:
Putting The Right Brains On The Right Trains

In the coming chapters, I will make frequent use of terms related to brain hemisphere dominance. People who are dominant in the left hemisphere of their brains, we'll call them left-brained, or left-brainers, tend to be more adept at analysis and calculation, thinking categorically and systematically—left-brained people might be inclined to be mathematicians, administrators, and planners (or CFOs.) People who are dominant in the right hemisphere, the right-brained, tend to be more creative, artistic, and synthesizing, more adept at seeing the big picture, finding novel perspectives and solutions, and predicting trends. It is clear to me that left-brained practitioners are being employed in right-brain positions in the Arab world, and that this misuse of talent is hampering growth. The right-brain visionaries are the leaders of tomorrow's world and they should be the leaders in formulating strategies for the future.

Keep CFOs out of Marketing

If a company in the Middle East places a former CFO as its CEO when that individual lacks a basic background in marketing, the company is doomed, if for no other reason than the simple fact that most CFOs reject anything but numbers. They tend to be extreme left-brainers who hold as their foremost aim attaining some sort of result the very next day, often without regard to that result's long-term consequences. The Chief Marketing Officer sits on the other end of the spectrum, always emphasizing planning for the long term. I earnestly suggest that in the case of the death of the CEO, that the company should hire a former CMO as its new CEO as long as that individual is a right-brainer. It is imperative to understand the simple thinking of most, not all, CFOs. Then too, most CFOs, though not all, have very little perception of what marketing means. In this era of innovation, if a company hires in the position of CMO a left-brainer CFO, the brand is doomed. The bottom line is that companies need to understand the function of marketing without the CFO being allowed to intervene with the CEO.

Most CFOs remind me of Aunty Nelma, that lady that always complains about every little thing that comes along. CFOs are diehard haters of marketing, and are a primary cause of the major catastrophe that most Arab companies face in terms of their brand losses. I may sound to you now as if I resent CFOs. The fact is, I don't. But I do believe they are very often the curse besetting marketing in any organization, and that in the failure of most brands the CFO believes he has a case to establish against marketing, especially when the CEO has hired a relative or a friend to be the CMO. It must be said that I have witnessed most CFOs playing major roles in many companies, and that I believe it is extremely near-sighted of companies to take that approach. CFOs are such left-brainers that they can't even envision their figures for the next few years. In such a case, as in many others, I recommend that all CFOs prior to joining any company at such a sensitive position should try to develop a simple understanding of marketing, or have their company offer them training classes that will support this basic understanding of marketing and the reasons why marketing does what it does.

I have seen too many CFOs coming to companies and ruining them or even driving them from existence due to the fact that they have to sit and talk about almost everything that doesn't concern them or their position. The discussion that follows conveys the reality of CFOs in the MENA region, and it explains why multinationals, by contrast, almost always employ CFOs who have a basic of understanding of what marketing is and its expectations and deliverables. It is most imperative that such a requirement be established among all local firms in the MENA region. You have to know what your expectations from your CFO are as far as his obligation to support the marketing department to reach and deliver its goals. The organization is not about the unit department. Rather, it is about people who work together in unified way to deliver a single goal for a single cause.

My God, if you, my readers, had experienced some of the things I have experienced, your heart would cry out, and you would ask along with me, "Why are these companies draining their resources and wasting their opportunities?" In most cases it is the CFO who winds up pulling the trigger on the bad decisions by influencing the CEO to make ill-informed but drastic changes. Then, when the brand fails, most CFOs just completely bail out of their responsibility and place the poor marketing guy in the line of fire. Most CFOs in my experience are the last to leave the company after they have drained the meaning out of it, and to their last day in the company they are sitting in their chairs blaming every other department.

A question I would have for business owners and CEOs is this: Do you think the quality of your CFO's car determines how much money your company makes? Most CFOs in the region only believe in keeping up their chair and wining and dining the owner and the CEO and not taking care of the company. There is an upcoming chapter more specifically on the interplay between CFOs and marketing. If you are a CEO who allows such a thing to happen, then simply put, you're not suited to run the company in the right direction. Your CFO must know that marketing is far too important to juggle with. Marketing is the reason for your brand to have cash flow. If you consider marketing to be unimportant in your role as CEO, then please fire yourself or submit your resignation, because you're just as clueless as anyone else would be in terms of your ability to run a company. Chairmen of the board, please make sure your CEO is a center-minded person, striking a balance between left and right, and certainly not just a left-brained person, or your organization will miss the opportunity to reach its peak into today's economy. If you hire a left-brained CEO, he will bring in a CFO, but one who is similar to him, so that everything is always left, and in that case, nothing is right! If you fail to do your duty in appointing a CEO with the right temperament and training to run the company, balancing the needs of the CFO and CMO, I hold you responsible for every mistake you and your CEO will make and the thousands who will lose their jobs because of your narrow self-interest.

Now my message on CFOs goes directly to the Chairman of trade organizations, to CEOs and to the rest of the gang: Please consider credentials in all top management positions, and consider that these positions are not for anyone to meddle with. Instead all must take responsibility as professionals to work as one with a similar mindset, toward a single and strive to bring the diversified cultures of the company into one. I recommend that companies endeavor to teach their CFOs a basic understanding of marketing so that they will be able to assess the deliverables and work closely with the marketing department, instead of merely opposing and blaming it. Business owners should make sure their CFOs are not extreme left-brainers who will only sit and judge everyone around them. Frequently CFOs seem to have the effect of dividing the company into two. By contrast, the marketing discipline believes in unity, because true marketers are visionaries. I would also recommend that CEOs consider that the CFO is not a jack of all trades. The CEO should assign him specific tasks within the limits of his duties and expertise, and try not to throw at him all the CEO's desires for magical results in terms of numbers.

Right-brainers for CEO!
With the world economy changing and more consumer-based markets emerging, the talk of the news and the hottest thing to consider in your business life is *brands*. Brands are the way to

the hearts of millions, and there is no way around this fact. This fact lives in almost every business in the world and in all sectors. One should consider the wave and not go against it; one should consider today's market demand and not one's own demands; one should continue to innovate and introduce new brands as often as the company can create new markets and new categories. In order to achieve these conditions, board members must accept that companies must be headed by CEOs who are right-brain marketers in order to achieve a competitive edge or to lead the company toward a new horizon. My reasons are more than the reality that such are the leaders who have attained the most striking results over the past decade. In terms of my recommendation that right-brained marketers should become CEOs, here are some reasons to consider if you are willing.

1. Today's markets are about ideas, innovation and creating categories; who is better at doing that than a right-brained marketer?
2. Today's market is about creating powerful brands; who's better at doing that than a right-brained marketer?
3. Today's marketing is about being competitive and managing expectations; who's better at doing that than a right-brained marketer?
4. Today's market is about creating expectations; who's better at doing that than a right-brained marketer?
5. Today's market is about having a long-term vision; who's better at doing that than a right-brained marketer?

Classic Examples of right-brained CEOs:

1. Steve Jobs of Apple was all about innovation and he was a right-brained marketer with a formidable talent

2. Richard Branson, the Virgin guru, represented by the brand and for the brand for all time. He is a right-brainer CEO who created the Virgin brand.

Branding our Way Forward

Brands are far more important than you and I; they can be a caretaker of many homes if they are done right. They are the face of your company; your name as owner comes last; the brand comes before you. Tomorrow's brands, those under the right management, are those that are brand-oriented to create the impact that the audience expects. Tomorrow's right management consists of brand-takers who have moved away from the classic uniform thinking of brand management that P&G adopted years ago and never changed. Tomorrow's brands under right management are led by those right-brainers who create an environment for the brand to live in and a culture for the brand away from the corporate culture that is a far remove from the brand drive. The corporate culture must be the brand-driven culture, and the two are indispensable as a force for the company. Considering this, then what drives the brand force? What brings the narrow-minded CEO or business owner to change his mind and accept today's changes?

Usually the needful change is made only when the company faces threats that are diminishing the brand. In such cases only a consultant, as I am in marketing, is called in to fix the mess. Do I accept? I usually do because I love the challenge, but I require certain criteria, and they are not negotiable if the brand is to regain its strength. Have I managed to make that happen before? Several times, yes, and sometimes I was robbed of the credit I deserved. However, things are different now. When dealing with clients in the region, I now set my rules up front and have them all in writing, and I keep my love for marketing at home. I control my emotions so they do not get in the way. Another problem is this: What happens after I fix things up? The same story takes place. The head of the operation tries to be smart and modify the strategy I have set down up front and the company loses ground again, and these days I refuse to go back to those same clients.

Tomorrow's brands must be managed under the right CEO and COO. Each one of these people is responsible for the total brand deliverables and for managing customers' expectations. Usually, however, the CFO pressures his line of marketing or sales to do as he pleases and the CMO fails in this conflict to a certain extent. I have hope that tomorrow's brands will be under proper management in the MENA region. But this will happen only if the right management comes into place under a right-brained marketer as CEO, and I see no second option to this.

We are an in era of visionaries. The management must be able to sustain growth through a mission of action to reach its objective within the first three years. The management must have good marketing knowledge and insight in order to able to make the right decisions and deliver on the shareholders' expectations. Unless this is done I can never foresee regional brands passing the border of Sudan or Yemen.

Companies should be focused on the micro level for the first few years with one eye open for a macro opportunity. We must not disregard the importance of brands and how they reflect on our company. If you, the CEO of tomorrow, wish to do well for yourself and your company, and if you happen to be the owner, too, please treat yourself as an employee and anticipate all the changes and accept them as they come. If you can't lead, then kindly step aside and let someone lead who will do your company good. In all circumstances, right thinking and the thoughts we put in with positive energy are what bring our brand to the top. If you feel you're not equipped with the needed experience, then resign from the post and do yourself and the company a big favor.

Chapter 9:
The Shape We're In

As we develop more of an idea about what needs to be done, it's important to keep an eye on how far we have to go. As we said at the beginning, acknowledgment is the first step of the brand revolution. To give readers an idea of exactly where we are and how far we have to go, and perhaps to inspire a bit of revolutionary fervor, this chapter concerns returns our discussion to some of the main forces holding back business in the Middle East

The Ego without the Experience

First on the list is a curious combination of arrogance and inexperience that seems to beset us. This is a disorder that seems to beset the business owners in our regions, the CEOs with no previous experience, and the heads of marketing who know little more than what a logo identity is. Such unqualified individuals in positions of power and influence are a reality we all live with every day, a reality in which numerous companies are operating without any form of experience in developing their strategies. The business owner will sit with his family and select the colors they would like on the logo, and the hired CEO will simply follow along, and the inexperienced CMO accepts things as they are and runs the show. The business owner comes from a trader's mindset, with experience in the import of goods and in distributing those goods to wholesalers and receiving cash the next day. The same cycle goes around for years, while the nature of the market continues to change. How many live and do business today in the same way they have since the 60s or 70s? Certainly it must be many.

The ego behind the ability of such business leaders to refuse to listen to an expert is a major problem that most companies in the Middle East either have faced or are still facing. The business owners are decisive, even when their decisions are ill-informed, and those decisions are then left to a few inexperienced people to act on them. The same applies to inexperienced first-time CEOs or even CMOs who refuse to change the brand nature and who even seem unwilling to try. How many such business leaders are there? If you scan the market today you will find a great many. Many of these people fear change because they fear incurring a loss, and because they lack confidence in their ability to run toward the necessary change and to capitalize on doing so.

A second group are the newcomers who have read a few books about how to run companies. These are the CEOs, CFOs and COOs who are still far from reality, and still living the ego life. They have probably watched several movies featuring handsome actors playing CEOs, and that Hollywood experience defined the job for them: to act as if they are large and in charge, and to be egotistic about the decisions that one must make when finally pressed to do so because one finally cannot simply ignore the need for a decision. The ego means that this person without prior experience running a company can begin making decisions that will reflect on the entire company and all its employees who are counting on the company for their living. It is simply totally obscure to me how this can happen. Such business owners must somehow come to their senses and admit their shortcomings, and then let the business be managed by someone who would do a much better job. I have encountered several cases in which the title of the position does not fit the criteria of the individual, and the result usually is a blunder.

Living the experience of being a CEO and enjoying all the little toys that come with the job, versus the experience of rolling up one's sleeves and doing the job are two very different functions. The first is composed of building a mere presentation of *to be* and the second one is defined by *action in motion*. Each of these purposes is distinct in every respect. The CEO who embraces the first purpose keeps the office warm and over-decorated and the second one walks the walk and talks the talk. The first one likes to read the newspapers all morning and drink tea while calling friends and chit-chatting, and the second one is running up and down on all floors of the building to ensure that the company is getting the leadership it needs. The first one is busy using up company resources for his own needs and those of his family, and the second one is making sure that the company policies apply to him as much as to the rest of the employees. The first may be missing a job description, but he is never without an expensive pen to use at any time for writing his signature. (He is very fond of his signature.) The second one has to see to all his paperwork before the day is over to ensure that the desk is clear for the next day's work. Finally, the first one clings to the arrogance of "how should we seem" while the second one holds the modesty of "let's produce."

So of these two people, who should be the CEO? I wonder! For the sake of the company, who should be the CEO? Please, someone, tell me which of the two would you prefer, the real or the imagined? How do we move forward if the CEOs governed by ego and the need to seem to be something they're not continue not just to exist, but to hold sway in the region? I wonder, then, whom I should consult? It could be that even the employees on the front lines would do a better job as CEOs because they are at least experiencing the company every day. I leave the rest to all of you to decide.

As a classic example, most recently one of my clients in the financial industry who is operating an organization that is doomed by his failures and who is continuing to pay himself and his walking soldiers a hefty salary just to protect his wisdom, came to the conclusion that his business development department was a failure, and fired the experts in it, and subordinated the communications department under the business development department because it was not a cost center (showing zero attention to brand investment or even toward adding value to the brand equity). He then hired one of his relatives to lead the communications department, supervised by two unqualified individuals who constantly failed. And most recently, he hired a person who has is so little qualified to run a department that he uses cooking recipes to give examples of models.

This was the joke of the century in my consulting career, and yet the CEO, or as he calls himself, "the executive director," failed to run the company into profit for five consecutive years, and his shareholders (yes, the company was publicly traded) were already sick and tired of the ongoing saga. Having all this in mind, the company fired most of its European and foreign executives due to disagreements over the path of the company and its direction. Second, the CEO shut down his two extended offices and claimed that the company was successful, at which point one of the offices was incepted and closed in just nine months. This story says a great deal about the wisdom of this individual and about the terms of his failure. The problem of this company was simply having him as the head of the company. In case my readers are wondering, I did address my concerns to the man, and told him that he should step down from his position. But for some reason he took it personally. In the end, I lost my final payment because I had disagreed with him and his new business development officer, who seemed to be a complete airhead, and who had landed this job based on favoritism and had insufficient previous experience in marketing to even operate a business development division. The failure of this CEO, or "executive director," will only lead to the failure of the company. I don't think this company will get anywhere in the near future. Its line of penetration is only networking, and that's an atmosphere too thin to operate in. With the change of generation HNWI families do change, and it seems likely their children will be able to manage such situations better. It's difficult to imagine they could do any worse.

Theories and Other Big Words

This is really hilarious to me: You go to a meeting and unfold exactly what a firm needs to do to be viable, and they dismiss it by saying it is all "just a theory." How often have you heard that phrase? Well, ladies and gentlemen, the West and the rest of the world create products and services every day based on theory and we are using them. Did we in the Middle East ever show up with our own theory? Perhaps our business leaders don't believe in theory. That's fine. Thanks to Procter and Gamble at least we have the knowhow to manufacture dippers. Apparently changing our nature from that of traders to that of business people is not as easy as it might seem.

Be that as it may, when someone in a position of business leadership is stuck in a trading mentality, no theory can ever go through their thick-headed, one mindset point of view. I hold this as a major issue in the MENA region. Given the difficulty of the business leadership in setting a course to the future on their own, we need case studies to be set in motion to discern whether our companies are heading in the right direction. Perhaps where theories can't work themselves into the trader's mindset, some persuasive numbers would.

Theories are a must. Without theories nothing could be created. Of those who have no faith in theory, I would ask how they would sustain growth with the current global change in terms of our economical nature, and the shift from West to East, and with the rise of the Internet as a must-have hub of trillion-dollar industries. Theories do matter, and those who fear them should stay home and keep their money in the bank, because they will never make a change in the community, though they will infest the community with their negative energy.

The corporate strategy, which encompasses the essential processes of a company, is a theory, and an important one at that. It is a vitally important set of ideas (as many theories are) that sustains a company as it travels in a single direction based on a strategic objective and a unified corporate initiative. To business owners who resist theory I would point out that without a corporate strategy your company is doomed, my friend. Furthermore, I am doing you an enormous favor when I tell you this: Don't go and just write a mission statement that has no other purpose than to look good on your profile and website. Your mission statement should be the vision by which you walk the walk and talk the talk to achieve your vision. But again, the subject of corporate strategy would require another book and much more time than we have here to address.

I am an advocate for marketing, and that, of course, also is a theory, but experience has shown that it is a tangible and workable theory. The external strategy of the corporation is most essential in developing a marketing strategy. Without the external strategy your marketing strategy direction will be totally out of plan. Ask yourself now, do theories matter? Can you run your company without theories? Without embracing some sort of theory and putting it into practice you will never witness your maximum profit. Take it or leave it: that's a fact you have to face even if you are the business owner or CEO. If you leave it, then you should perhaps also face the fact that you are probably not well-equipped to run a company based on a corporate strategy, because that, being a theory, will also apply to you. So what is it that you want? A company, or a set of big words you can enjoy using in front of friends at gatherings, when you probably don't even know what they mean?

Allow me to offer a pertinent example: The COO I mentioned in the first chapter works at an automotive dealers in the MENA region, and he is basically a clueless man who suffers from the most acute case of uncommonly low self-esteem. This gentleman has caused his company enormous losses, to the extent that one of the auto brands that he represents lost its presence in the country he is operating in. The guy leaves his office and goes on trips just to shop and dress up, having no clue how to even dress to begin with. But he is a diehard want-to-be Italian (An ambition driven by his want-to-be Italian fake wife). This gentleman had the habit of imagining theories and then calling his staff and telling them he had read up on marketing and that he was a strategist. One day he declared himself a management strategist after reading the Jack Welch book *Winners*. How in the world could such a COO still hold his position merely based on his enjoyment of applying big words to himself? Such responsibility as is embodied in the position of COO should not be a mere presentation of want-to-be, it should be as simple as motion in action. For God's sake, it's the operation of a company.

To such men I would like to say this: Big words are only big words: Use them if you know their meaning and you are able to apply them appropriately in your models. Theories are things we should not ignore, because theories are what we are able to use to shape our future as a company and as a nation. Our thoughts are theories, and every step we take was a theory before it became an action. So think how important theories are in our lives. Think of what your company needs and not about what you need. Think of how far your company has to go, and be competitive, and stop worrying about your shopping and your cars, and think about the reality of what you will leave behind for your family, community, and nation, and not about your leisure time. Consider the mistakes you made and why you made them. Accept these mistakes modestly and move forward into a brighter future based on your ability to learn from your own past.

Theories are the means by which we have progressed in this world. Look at everything around you that you love: It was a theory at one point in before you enjoyed using it. Think and act accordingly. Part of theory is to accept those who are better than you at a specific task, and who can do their business a lot better than you could. They have the ability to develop theories into models and then apply them to consumer experience. But you don't. So accept it. Accept that big words are only big words that only serve to show your presence, but when it comes to the real deal, when you're tested, then you will have to defer to those who taught you those words, and who actually know their meaning because they have real-world experience. Your marriage was out of a theory—out of love—or perhaps it was out of the theory of arranged marriages for their purposes and reasons. The power of theory applies everywhere, and not only in your office but also in your home. Do you have any procedures and policies? That's a theory, but it is one which is implemented within guidelines. Do you use a Key performance indicator? If you don't believe in theory, then why use it? It is a theory, too.

Stop saying "just a theory"! Theories work, but they need experienced individuals to carry out the necessary tasks and supply tangible deliverables that account for company growth. And not everyone can work on theories, only a few who have experienced doing so and achieved results. So, Arab business owner or executive, set yourself aside, reshuffle the mess you have created, and hire properly credentialed employees. And if you have relatives who work for you and are not qualified, fire them all and make sure they get a job somewhere else to earn and compile experience. Experience makes people better. The late Steve Jobs turned lots of theories under his "I" categories into tangible, real products and definitely carried out his mission and vision very well, as you can tell from his positioning. *Think different!* Apple is the king of hatching theories that turn things into reality. Apple is the effect of a theory hatched by a right-brainer CEO who envisioned the future far ahead of his peers. Apple enjoys the theory world that changed the life of the company after Steve Jobs took office as CEO and fired the Pepsi guy. Who can argue about Apple today? Apparently, *you!* Think twice; maybe you need to look at your company and face reality. First of all, you're using Apple products. May I ask, is Apple using your products and services? No? So face reality, buddy, and park your Armani suit in the closet and make sure you sleep well. Please be honest with yourself.

Have you ever spent time in your office as a business owner and CEO and wondered where you went wrong? Did you admit, at least to yourself, that you were responsible for the time wasted because your ego got in the way? Did you ever sit and separate your personal needs from the company's needs? Did you ever sit and wonder why you abused your employees and took advantage of them? Did you ever take any advice from a right-brained marketer, or on the contrary, did you recognize he was right, but again couldn't admit your ego was in the way? Who is more important, you or the brand you created? Who brings the cash to your CFO, the brand or you and your CFO? If you are able to answer these questions modestly and to submit to the truth, then you've taken the first step in right management for tomorrow's brand.

P&G, Unilever: Great Success, Bad Examples

A great part of the Middle Eastern marketing and advertising culture was brought into the region by multinationals such as P&G and Unilever and others. By a strange twist of events, this type of culture of mass-moving consumer goods is part of what inclined the market toward being advertising-driven instead of marketing-oriented, even though these multinationals clearly know their marketing, and do it well. The attraction of these companies for local businesses is that P&G and Unilever hold categories all across the board that local manufacturers have left void for years, having never bothered to produce in those categories before the international players came in. However, in the final analysis, the P&G culture of marketing in the region is far from the true essence of marketing or brands.

The key thing to understand in this regard is that even though such multinationals are enormously successful, their success in the region is not contagious to other businesses, even when local businesses hire away Arab executives trained and seasoned in those corporations. This is because all multinationals in our region are operating at the execution level and not at the strategic level. All of the strategy—the product development and marketing design—is developed elsewhere, either in the corporations' home countries or at the Global Business Unit (GBU) in Switzerland.

One can see the attractiveness for a Middle Eastern company of bringing on a successful executive from one of those multinationals to head a division of a local business, but local CEOs should face the fact: not every brand manager from multinationals can be a director of marketing given a bit of classic brand management experience and market research. These things account for only a small percentage of what marketing is. The classic style of brand management that was introduced by McElroy in the early 1930s, such as the famous Camay Ad, a line that is used to this day, are international brands, merely managed by local brand managers and directors of marketing, all left-brainers, and mostly engineering graduates, curiously, because it is in the best interest of these multinationals to look for people to execute and not to think. This analysis applies across the board to all multinational brands, not just the P&G brands.

The other point to bring to the table is this: Brands that have already operated for years, some for a century, have already shown a record of success and are innovative within their industries. Nevertheless most of these brands of the multinationals operating in the region are need products and convenience products, for which the market demand dictates the supply for each product category leadership. My main argument here is that the process of marketing in P&G and other multinationals is organized, structured marketing with the highest expectations of deliverables, a process far distant from what the process, structure and expectations are in each of the home countries of these brands. The MENA region is merely the execution level, at which these multinational brands adapt the brand to local habits and conceptions and supply local manufacturing, while the raw materials and design are imported from the brand's home country. This is a great model, and it has worked well across the world, so that today P&G is one of the world's most respected conglomerated sub-brand producers, as is Unilever.

The crux of my argument is that there is a confusion in the region between a real structured marketing department accredited by marketers experienced in strategies and thinking versus the daily brand management execution on simple models of A, B, C and D put together by engineers.

This culture simply spread intact to local firms to allow these individuals to hold high posts as directors of marketing, although they had only brand management experience. Some have succeeded; others have completely failed. For example, the local Goody's brand is a category filler in Saudi Arabia, and has a done a great job in brand recognition and product distribution. The Goody's brand holds plenty of SKU's, and we could also say that it is a focused brand in the sense of category. The company holds one of the most well-detailed distribution channels in the region, and its brand presence has been well observed across all levels of income groups. It is obvious that the brand is managed under a P&G-style culture, and yet what supports it are two very dependable lines: A) Constant improvement of channels of distribution through the art of merchandizing and B) Constant brand recognition building on all sub-products. My one concern would be the brand line extension if ever Goody operates in a very strongly cluttered category.

In the war of the energy drinks between local brands and imported brands, a local firm that produces locally branded beverages with enormous potential approached me for my consultancy on an energy drink in the Kingdom of Saudi Arabia. This local brand never had the P&G marketing culture and was less organized than I expected, but as I said, it had great potential. My offer to consult was very simple: I requested that the network of channels should be improved and that they should have a goal within the kingdom. Second, I told them to break away from the product profile color of silver and blue and do a flashy red, and to initiate a policy of price competitiveness. These points brought Code Red to life, using the red of Red Bull as the primary color of the can; today Code Red is a leading energy drink in the kingdom over the past five years with little more than $30,000 spent on advertising. Now, you don't see much brand management in this case study, but it is full of tactical strategy and brand strategy.

In clearing up the confusion created by the success of the multinationals in the region, my point is as simple as what I have stated above: advertising is nothing but a reach of communication that is somewhat important in early brand-building recognition, while marketing is what should assume the role of consumer penetration and building brands. The multinational culture of brand management and the advertising-driven approach are only good for those multinationals which are established brands elsewhere, but not for incoming local brands that are still trying to penetrate the local market and maintain a presence. Marketing is a process of strategy and planning and being on constant alert to keep the brand engaged, but if you depend only on brand management for market deliverables, then you have a problem. That approach is good, but the fact is that each of the brands differs from the other in their nature. Our local consumers in the region seem only to trust the important brands because they are managed well and do leave an impact as compared to the local brands that think distribution, sales and advertising will attain them their desired result. Such behavior I have vigorously fought against for years within the region, with the result in most cases that my arguments are only heard, and are only accepted, after the brand faces its inevitable but apparently unforeseen fate.

Me-too brands

"Me-too" is an advertising term commonly applied to a brand which replicates an established brand's distinctive look and feel. For example, a soft drink maker might market something that looks like a Pepsi, with the same colors and brand icon but a different name. This kind of replication is quite ubiquitous in the regional market. The point is that most CEOs or business owners in the region believe that they can score a quick success simply by creating a me-too brand and reducing the price to a competitive level.

I have a rather direct response to that strategy: How in the hell are you going to do that? One brand's successes cannot be duplicated, as I have mentioned above. The thought of laying out an enormous investment only to create a me-too brand is just incredible. A business plan is a rare commodity to find in these new ventures. Business plans are similarly rare to find in any trade-oriented organizations as compared to a structured business organization. With this in mind, what would be the rescue process for these trade organizations that generally speaking don't even believe in theories or the most simple planning paperwork, but strongly believe in replicated models of brands that already exist, produced by international firms?

Why me-too brands? Why replicate? Perhaps there are safety reasons for the "entrepreneur," due to the fact that one instance of the product has succeeded and showed a proven record of achievement. But would that same formula really work for a second and third similar brand operating in the same category based only on this thin perception?

All these are vital questions to consider when taking on the task of a me-too brand. If you're a CEO or a business owner, then sit with yourself and consider the above questions and finally ask yourself how long your me-too brand could sustain itself in terms of brand management, unless it also plans to replicate the brand's metaphors.

The simplest of marketing insights could help entrepreneurs avoid this no-win situation. Consider, for instance, how me-too brands would work when contemplated under the concept of product category. For one thing, how do you ever hope to make headway in a category when you begin by acknowledging another brand's superiority in that category? A me-too product brands itself as a failure the second it makes its appearance. By contrast, the brands that innovate a category tie that category strongly to the name of their brands. A classic example: In most cases when you ask for a tissue you ask for a Kleenex. The innovating brand name is the one that comes to people's minds. The same applies when you want to photocopy a document. Often, you say you want to Xerox it. Each of these two brand names is the dominant leader in its category, and these brands remain for-sure cash generators. Considering these points, an entrepreneur would do well to strive to create a category, and not merely copy a brand in an established category, especially when the category is named after the product. The plan to penetrate via the simplistic strategy of a price war is simply a failed strategy in most cases.

Instead, what you can do is diverge from the category and create your own. Categories are the heart and art of marketing strategies. You must obtain and maintain a very creative mind to push forward with this sort of effort. If you cannot, then consider hiring a brand marketing strategy consultant like me to make the difference with your brands. You must consider that marketing is a lot more than simply sales and advertising; marketing is the heart of the entire brand life process. It is the organ of your business that keeps it functional.

My recommendation on the me-too brand is to please avoid it; don't get close to it; you cannot sustain a business that is looked upon as a copy of the original. No matter what you do, the consumer's mind is almost impossible to change once he has experienced all the negative impacts that the brand has possessed. Try to avoid this trouble, try to go back to basics and develop a proper business plan and understand the market and its categories before you enter them. Consider "I don't know" a blessing. You should be modest and bring in those who know what they're doing to do the job for you. Having an expert on your side is always a guideline for every step you take. Do not engage in a me-too concept; it is a no way out deal. Also consider that any advertising agency that you deal with should be in the presence of a marketing consultant or someone experienced in the industry. Stop the bleeding and please pass along this advice to friends who are in the business or family, and you will be blessed too.

The Advertising Money Pit

The union between the brand and the consumer is marketing, and not advertising. One of the factors in the Middle East context that holds individual companies and the entire region back is an unreasonable and unhealthy dependence on advertising as the primary means of advancing a product line. This is a problem that is compounded in our context by unscrupulous and sometimes unethical advertising companies that seek to perpetuate and cash in on that reliance. Marketing holds all the answers to every consumer's questions, and not advertising, and the failure to acknowledge this fact is the trap that most CEOs and business owners fall into, until eventually the brand declines.

CEOs be warned: If the advertising agency develops a me-too brand and recommends it to you, then consider that this advertising agency is unethical and only out for a buck. In many cases you need to also check around the region concerning some of the communications ideas you're receiving. Some of the advertising agencies replicate ideas from international brands and present them as original to the client, and that in itself is an act of a me-too branding on the part of the agency. Consider professionalism and a respect for intellectual property to be part of your way of doing business and consider that once you have a business plan the rest will come along.

The continuing saga of most advertising agencies is a matter of how the account value is, and how much they plan to support the client spending on all media channels, plus the agency fees. Where did the true story of the advertising agency go? The advertising agency used to be as good as a ticketing agency, expecting 17.5% agency fees for channeling. Then came the art of visual communication, TV, and print in terms of production. Now, some agencies have begun to claim to offer a brand strategy and marketing strategy. To me, these agencies are jacks of all trades and masters of none, such that the agencies have become more like supermarkets, either a one-stop solution or a shop-and-spend. What happened to the true advertising agency's job of supporting communication and developing the visuals based on brand essence and attributes? The agencies have also begun to enter the public relations agency area, though I am relieved that there remain some specialized PR agencies. It's difficult to predict what might be next for these agencies.

The hardcore advertising-believer CEOs, plenty of them, have paid the price of losing their brand objectives because they have assumed that advertising will return their investment. The first mistake of these CEOs and business owners is that they have never made the effort to understand what marketing is before their engagement with advertising agencies. Most are simply trend followers who believe only in the fellowship and not the leadership. So, of the business owners and CEOs I would ask, how much was your advertising budget this year? How much did you spend? Did you make the sales you expected? If you counted primarily on advertising for increasing your sales, then I can answer that question for you. You did not.

Never was it the case that advertising was the end solution for brand expectations or deliverables. In fact, advertising has been a burden in many or most cases in our region. Although the agencies have frequently tried to play the role of marketer, you can expect from this art that you commission precisely that you will communicate the brand and nothing more. Yes, in most cases advertising is just art. Many MENA advertising agencies have led many companies into a fatal result, and by that I mean they have caused companies to shut down. In most cases the advertising agencies have made a name for themselves through worldwide reputable brands, such as those branded by the multinationals we discussed above, and they attain these accounts not based on credentials, but by networking through friends. Hiring friends is fine, but only if the friends are qualified.

Once these agencies take off, however, boy, do you see an ego. The agencies act not only as advertisers but also as PR and everything they can even vaguely associate with advertising. They try to present themselves as market gurus although they actually know little of marketing. Nor do I think they are often even very good at advertising. I have seen a great many brands depend on a woman as a connection to the audience. Why? The idea that women attract men? I suppose a brand is a brand, but in most cases so many ads in the region have fallen in on the trend and gone in that direction without addressing proper brand positioning that the effort seems pointless. The strategy, if you can call it that, has been rendered practically invisible by repetition.

So, business owner or CEO, how much did you spend this year on advertising? Did you get back what you spent or merely get to admire the beautiful ads as you shared them with your friends and family? The truth is that no matter how much your budget for advertising is, if there is no proper marketing process, plan or strategy, then please save yourself the money and put it into direct marketing or even into brand activation. These activities I truly believe in, because they have the ability to bring the customer to the experience of the brand. Consider many factors before throwing your budget away or handing it over to advertising agencies to do with as they please. The point of advertising is to support marketing at the communication level of all product lines and to build brand recognition through the media channels per the brand attributes. In other cases, when advertising agencies deliver only as they wish and act as if they were gurus of the market, that's when the brand comes to trouble.

It is a circus to me, all lights and glitter, when an advertising agency tries to come in and promise the CEO that it will increase its sales. How would advertising do that? Brad Pitt? Will Smith? Well, they are great brand icons but their role in the local region is expensive. Then what? Run a circus down the street consisting of 50,000 dancers wearing a t-shirt that bears the brand name? Grand promises should not be made by an advertising agency that is far distant from the reality of the market and consumer expectations. Advertising agencies should avoid promising to offer all one's branding and publicity needs over the counter and they should focus on the one thing they do well, the thing that is the purpose of their existence, and that is to support the marketing through a communication platform. They should not to try to act as the marketing arm of the organization. The empty promises that are thrown out by a few non-reputable advertising agencies have damaged the industry's image as whole. Even now a few of the public relation agencies hate to be associated with advertising because of the backlash that the industry has experienced in recent years.

The advertising agencies must realize the threats to the industry, and work on rebuilding the industry in accord with its true essence, and avoid running it in too many directions. I believe also that the world advertising body should look into the industry's problems in the region and address their findings to the local agencies. I hope that advertising will stay away from the face of marketing and only be the arm that moves when it is needed.

So, business owners and executives, think always before you decide on what action to take, and ask if you don't know. I recommend that you use advertising only under the supervision of your marketing department or consultant and not based on your personal attributes. I would also advise you to take a moment of your time and read up on marketing or ask someone to explain to you what marketing is rather than just face the problem you're facing alone. Think and act professionally with your staff and deliver what is expected of you as the CEO of the company rather than making yourself the face of the company. Think of your brand and spend some time to understand your brand prior to thinking that advertising will do the right job for you. Think and see what will take your brand to be a brand if it is still struggling. Look at the right guidelines, ask experts and don't try to be an expert and fail.

Consult experts. The cost of doing otherwise is horrendous, and if you make the right decision now you will be able to avoid that cost simply by acknowledging what you know and what you don't know. Accept the truth as the CEO and business owner that advertising spending is not the right direction for your brand. Consider studying categories and see how they operate. Hold yourself responsible for the firm you operate or own and look carefully for the best interests of your organization and its expectations. Spending millions on advertising was never the solution. Spending a much more reasonable amount on marketing is the solution.

Chapter 10:
The CEO Problem Revisited

The specter of all these various drags on our businesses and economy bring us back to the CEO as the center point of the problem. I'd like to spend a chapter talking specifically about the problems we face with our CEOs in an attempt to perhaps shake some people awake, before I lead us to some sources of hope. Over the past eleven years, I have seen enormous brand failure due to the fact that most CEOs fail to allow themselves to be coached on marketing or even to consult experienced marketing consultants or advertising agencies. In my case, I have experienced the same pattern of questions from most CEOs: "How long until my investment will become commercially viable?" My answer is always the same: "That depends on the management's commitment to the task." Most shareholders and CEOs fail to understand that eight percent of their company value is their brand and that although this form of value might not appear on paper, it nonetheless seems to be an established fact, and one of the main reasons investment bankers and brokers are attracted to companies who have demonstrated that they are willing not only to produce products and desire to make money, but that they are ready to be responsible for their brand.

In what follows perhaps I will sometimes seem to be taking these matters lightly by addressing them with a sense of humor.

But if there's any humor, it is a grim armor. In truth I am speaking from deep within in my heart, in words informed by the agony of experience. Remember, this is not merely the death of a business that concerns me, or a lapse in marketing. It's a potential employer of my people no longer being viable. It's another blow to the reputation of my business community. And business failures cause actual suffering to many people. It sometimes seems to me that the CEOs and owners are the only ones who sometimes manage not to suffer.

The ongoing problem, as we have discussed, is that positions are given not based on credentials but based on who knows who and whether the person hired is a friend or family member. The title of CEO is hand-thrown to anyone that it may suit the owner to have in the position, such that the title is like giving any name you like to anything you like. Earlier I have spoken about CEOs and their roles, and whether the job description applies to them or not. All this discussion emerges from what I have experienced in the Middle East. The old-minded CEOs fail to grow or perhaps even avoid attaining constant growth amid changes in the market, in favor of settling for what they know best.

The Rattled Chair CEOs

These are the funniest CEOs, and when they are family members, you can imagine that the title was simply bestowed and plastered on a business card, as they were placed in a lavish office that probably cost more than one hundred thousand dollars to decorate. A mahogany armchair sits behind the desk, and accessories adorn it which have been chosen by his fashion advisor. A bookshelf stretches from one end of the wall to the other collecting dust. The only thing that is missing from the office, apart from something to fill the empty desk drawers, is a proper job description that goes with the title and responsibility. Many fail to understand their jobs, but remain busy, making very authoritative decisions that change the course and the life of the company, sometimes steering it from consistent performance to its downfall. Cost-cutting is one major step frequently executed, and this so-called decisive moon actually sometimes consists of firing all the high-paid and thus often the most qualified employees and replacing them with low-pay employees. And there you go the rest of the scene the reader may compose him or herself. You can easily imagine the result. These types of CEOs are holding their positions merely out of self-interest. Meanwhile, the evolution of the company in terms of taking the next step into the future revolves around them. They control the company with the deep-seated expectation that employees' commitment will be to them personally, and not to the company.

How will our brands ever flourish if such CEOs continue to exist and even hold sway in the heart of our business process? What will these incompetent CEOs do in order to move tighter in and merge with the emerging market of the BRIC states, rather than just committing themselves to the Western companies who need enormous help to sustain themselves at present? The rattled chair CEOs are those who have assigned themselves to the position just because they own the company. The result is usually a struggle; we find non-policy oriented companies managed based on PR and deciding what should be announced in the market based on their personal preferences. These individuals are well in tune with their low self-esteem, which finds them seeing to their personal needs for a veneer of respect and dignity at the cost of the well-being of the company. If they are employed by a company as a CEO because of friends of friends, they may abuse the power given to them and use the company out of personal interest, simply milking the concern dry to cater to personal family needs. It is sad to be in a position to have to discuss such things, but they are true.

I have seen the financial damage that can be inflicted by such incidents. A woman not too distantly related to me was married to the COO of a company or may be still married to him, God only knows. The gentleman abused the company for his personal needs and those of his wife. The position was given to him as a family member, but he most assuredly failed to even run the company at a level of basic competence, meanwhile firing anyone who dared question his motives. The rattled chair CEOs are best at keeping the chair warm and running up their phone bills and remaining clueless as to what the company is doing and what performance is expected.

The Rise of the Ego: The Fall of the Brand

At times the CEOs of the Middle East fail to accept change because it threatens their egos. Not only that, they resist opening their eyes to the truth, and they tend to reject any attempts to reason with them or correct their mistaken perceptions or assumptions. To my surprise I have even seen their threatened egos growing further still after they completely flop. Never do these men seem to come to their senses, and be modest, and accept that they have failed. In many cases the first reaction of these CEOs in terms of fixing a problem is to sit with friends and family and take suggestions which may be far from marketing reality, and which may be in the nature of the family group striving to tell the CEO what he wants to hear. Perhaps his driver may suggest changing out the company's management, or his daughter may suggest that he should change the brand colors, or his son, who was just appointed the COO of the firm, may take some liberties in making perilous decisions and throw the blame for their failure on his front-liners.

Did I ever witness these sorts of circumstances? Oh, God, yes. I have witnessed a person who has no clue as to what a CEO is became a CEO just by luck. Perhaps someone would raise the example of Mark Zuckerberg, founder of Facebook, as someone who is a successful inexperienced CEO, and many others like him, but these are people in the first place, who were innovators rather than followers, and second, people who tend to quickly admit to their shortcomings and hire advisors to guide them in their decisions. And when we talk about advisors in these circumstances, it must be remembered, we are talking about professional advisors with vast experience in the industry. In the Middle East, by contrast, owners tend to hire their best friends as advisors, or they may hire a cousin. I know that may sound funny to many readers, but this funny reality has been a fundamental operating fact for a great many brands that have completely failed due to a handful of people who truly believe that their money is their money, and that they may do as they wish. They have apparently never stopped to think that whatever damage is done to the company or the reputation of the brand also reflects on the image of his country and community, and on other people trying to do business in the region.

Many of the firms I have encountered have failed due to personal interests of the owners controlling the conduct of the company's business. Thus, the question will always remain as to how long the paradigm of unenlightened self interest will continue, even as the brands continue to fall apart one after the other. The expensive offices are not buying the skills that the job demands, and if these owners and CEOs don't get themselves in gear and take full responsibility for what the job expectations are, or what they ought to be, then the whole thing will hit rock bottom in no time.

The classic situation in the Middle East in business is sickeningly repetitive: You will find a CEO pushing his own image further than he pushes the brand. In many cases the CEO or business owner seeks constant publicity more than he seeks it for the brand by far. I would understand if this decision were based on personal branding and associating an identity with the company's performance, but many seem not to care about the business much; they merely focus on their personal objectives.

So why have we witnessed the fall of the brand and the rise of the CEO? Because in many cases CEOs, who are also commonly the business owners, are primarily considered with exploiting the media to showcase their names and hobbies and to wrangle invitations to speak about subjects they are utterly distant from in reality. So what comes first, Mr. Brand or Mr. CEO? The CEO should be the last on the list, because successful organizations work bottom-up and not top-down.

The CEO That Fell Asleep

The marketing department and the advertising agency have decided on the path of the product and the CEO is so completely caught up in the hierarchy that he won't go down to the bottom level to see outcomes and performance to indicate whether the direction of this product line is correct and aligned with his marketing strategy. Instead, he sits in his office and receives guests all day and discusses nonsense subjects. While the CEO is out of the picture and in the absence of a marketing strategy consultant or even just an advisor, the marketing manager with a little experience in advertising decides to execute with the ad agency all the hype the brand needs. Where is the CEO? He is in his own world, waiting for things to be done and then to appear and speak.

A few months later, after the launch of the brand and its fatal result, the CEO decides to fire the advertising agency that milked the brand and fire the marketing manager at the same time. In his press conference he announces that the marketing guy and the advertising agency ruined all his plans. Where was he? What was he doing? What was so important that kept him away?

Do CEOs snore over marketing presentations?

CEOs do often try to ignore the fact that they have overlooked pure marketing in their process. In many cases they see this, but again they only ignore what their mind rejects and neglect its importance. Many CEOs in our region are very left-brained. They are generally not receptive to new ideas or to change. What appeals to them are visual images driven only by perception, and not by the actual business model and its objectives. They tend to simply ignore the fact that they don't know, and admitting that fact is one of the most challenging efforts they could ever exert. Bearing this in mind, I would say that if the mind is accepting mere presentation or if a delusional force has taken over the mind, then the person has to live in the scenario *as if.* Given the chance and acceptance of failure they try to remodel the product based on personal instinct and ignore comprehensive marketing insights. In most cases the marketing department is left out of the process and the show is managed by non-marketers, the CEO, CFO and COO, all left-brainers. The resulting damage renders any brand that was intended unable to breathe or have a chance to live. Such disasters take place often in the Middle East. Business leaders should take the responsibility and be fired by the board, but they are clever in avoiding blame, a common disease within the region.

Chapter 11:
Toward Solutions

Is there a solution to the current problems, especially those centered on the CEOs? Absolutely—I have some serious solutions which I would like to pinpoint, and it is my sincere hope these points will somehow find their way to and by some miracle be accepted by the old-folk CEOs who are running these companies.

Acknowledgment and Acceptance

The first order of business is to bring people to acknowledge that the old days or the classic models used in the middle part of the last century are impossible to continue to observe and do business under today. Certainly they provide no means for moving a company into a position of market leadership. The lay of the land has changed, market operations have changed, people have changed in terms of their desires and tastes, there are more communication channels than ever, there are more industries and categories than ever before, and the list goes on and on. Perhaps among the most important changes is that the Internet is one of the strongest growing tools in the Middle East, one now virtually ignored by many business owners. Emerging markets are looking forward to developing their brands and engaging in strategies to penetrate the markets of the Western world.

The CEO Solution: Replace Yourself

Where do most or our CEOs stand in the middle of all this? Nowhere! They are off riding the caravans of our ancient dreams. Solution number one, as simple as it may sound, is as follows: If the old-minded refuse to acknowledge and adapt to current trends, then they should give up their seats to incoming potential CEOs or hire one rather than giving the chair up to their sons, who may have no clue whatsoever as to how to operate a firm. They could also hire a proxy CEO that could run the business much better than they can. The important thing is that the business owner should move to accept the fact that he is limited to an unproductive mindset.

It is of absolutely paramount importance that business owners remove their personal and family affairs from the roof of the company and treat themselves as employees according to law, and according to the best interests of the company. If you're failing as CEO, business owner, the wisest and most respectable decision, and in the long term the one that will reflect on you the best, is to fire yourself and give the job to someone who can do it. You should seriously consider whether you want to do your company and its employees any good, or if you would prefer to maintain an imagined status. The following steps are a must:

A. Hire people with credentials that indicate they will attain results for the company
B. Check into applicable laws to ensure everyone's protection
C. Develop a system of procedures and policies
D. Develop a proper corporate strategy that can drive the business toward results
E. Believe in marketing (Make sure that your new CEO has a clue as to what marketing is.)
F. Create a brand, believe in it, and let it attain for you the cash result you forecasted.

If we begin by considering the above points then at least we are heading down the right path into the business light, and our goals and returns will start to become clear for the following several years.

The Face of Change

In the past few months as I have been writing this book the Arab world has witnessed a new spring of change occasioned by the public who had their thoughts dictated to them since the day they were born as to what to do and say. Today in a few of the countries, the air of change has spread. Most people now feel that they have been reborn into a new world of what is right, and to the right of free speech. Such change has opened doors for more changes within the region. In the case of business I am absolutely sure that the change is bringing with it a new revolution from the trading mentality to the world of branding, a revolution for the current regional CEOs in terms of the change they should adopt to sustain the growth of our potential brands. These steps are more important than those steps that one must always climb on the ladder of change in our business world, in the absence of the necessary fundamental changes. Failing to make those necessary changes can only bring that future to a complete halt and the upcoming potential of change will dim.

Our Young CEOs

The future looks bright for incoming generations of CEOs—the young who are launching their own start-up companies or who have taken over their family businesses and are working to get them into shape. Some of these young incoming CEOs face the trouble, however, that they are inclined to simply follow what their forefathers practiced, fearing that change will precipitate an enormous decline from what has been built. The fact is that these young CEOs who are active for change, and who can see that change will bring globalization to a stagnant market, have a voice for their brands and can sense that their brands will allow for proper cash flow. These young CEOs in our region are also setting up properly structured firms, while the old-school CEOs resist making any changes. They resist change even though their direct consumers' needs are changing through the generations.

The fact is this: these young incoming CEOs are highly motivated and are speaking today's business language. If these next-generation entrepreneurs can learn the lessons that today's business world has to teach them in terms of proper financial departments and marketing, then one day our region will hold a strong stake in the global economy. I strongly count on these young entrepreneurs to make a difference and ensure that our brands will someday flourish around the globe. Young CEOs are the hope of tomorrow for our brands to flourish in the global market, but they must be heard and continue to have the courage to do what's good for the region. It may very well be that the call to action I issued above can only be executed by the incoming generations of CEOs, while the old school CEOS will do their best service for the region and for their businesses if they simply take a break and allow the generations to make their change at this crucial time of the world of globalization.

Those few who are not aware and blindly follow the old system, inherited through generations, will see their companies downsize from five thousand employees to one hundred employees—due to the fact that the changing world was not accounted for in their plan to remain stagnant, which, let's be frank, may scarcely be said to be a plan at all.

Today we also see young CEOs at a regional level promising to change how we conduct our marketing efforts. These select members of the future generation are primarily involved in start-up operations of midsize companies. Others are blending into the massive operations run by their fathers and forefathers.

The Need for Official Oversight and Support

An association or a governing body that oversees the entire region's potential and produces guidelines for small businesses and midsize corporations to refer to is not in place. How can we expect our businesses to thrive if no one understands the importance of establishing the fundamentals as a key to building up all the necessary elements to support the regional entrepreneurs in their endeavors? Such a long-term question can be expected to take days and months of discussion in order to get the proper wheels rolling, but I still beg to ask the question, how could things improve when the region holds the least number of organizations in the world to conduct workshops?

How can the region improve when most of the organizations to support business are merely based on personal whims and preferences? I have asked this question in the highest circles for many years, and yet I have always received the runaround, because a few people hate change due to the fact that their basic interests will be removed from the forefront, and because most then in power and privilege would lose control and fall behind. In order for marketing and branding to gain a foothold in the region, we must take official, collective action.

First, we must establish a regional marketing association that will assist brand owners in fulfilling their potential. This association would also refer brand owners to professionals who can assist with brand building and find models that will benefit the owners and their companies within a larger spectrum.

We must start from home base in all industries and initiate an oversight panel. Let's work together to enable our market to flourish. I am asking for everyone's involvement—from all countries in our region—in order to set up this association that will help us penetrate all possibilities for our brands.

We are a well-equipped society with enormous potential. Deploying a marketing association of the sort I envision might be difficult at first. But there is always a starting point, and perhaps that start will be sparked by something people read in this book. We have the manpower, the financials and the institutions to succeed. We are better off than a great many regions throughout the world. What we are missing appears to be the initiative to begin to do something and the guidelines by which to proceed intelligently.

Second, I sincerely suggest that we first redefine the meaning of "marketing" in Arabic and move away from the word *Tasweeq*, since its ambiguity does not help in its effectiveness. *Tasweeq* merely implies shopping, sales and getting products off the shelves. Redefining the meaning of marketing, first by means of finding a better word for it in the language, is a first step in the right direction.

Third, we should add a marketing major to the curricula of our universities as an alternative to general business administration majors.

Fourth, we should encourage community involvement and create public awareness of what marketing is, its purpose, and its value.

Fifth, and finally, it will take every firm, every marketer and every organization to move forward as a team so that one day we as Arabs will realize the dream of having our brands visible in the lives of all global consumers, on a par with competitive foreign multinationals.

If we can pull together and manage all this, then we will see growth and a complete change in how we think of marketing in terms of what it is, and the crucial role it plays in our organizations.

A Marketing Call to Action

As the reader may have observed, I am a passionate marketing advocate whose primary goal is to see any one of our consumer brands on supermarket shelves around the globe. But this will never happen unless those in the local market accept the responsibility for educating themselves on the basic principles of marketing. While the concept of brand positioning was created by Al Rise and Jack Trout some 20 years ago, it has only reached our region comparatively recently, and many marketers and ad agencies have yet to adopt the full principles of positioning. This situation demonstrates exactly how far behind we are in adapting and transforming. We begin to see how dangerous our circumstance is in terms of ensuring the prosperity of our companies and our people when we consider how far off we are, especially in this era of globalization, when many brands are perfectly synchronized within one point or place through such emerging avenues as ecommerce. Never mind "emerging." In most of the world ecommerce has thoroughly come on the scene. Just not in this region. Will the next generation of young marketers face these changes proactively, and recognize the potential financial rewards that follow? Here is my succinct call to action:

At this point, I address primarily all Arab business owners, of small and large scale firms alike, regarding the essential function of marketing in their companies. I urge you to take chances and enlighten yourselves about marketing concepts. This is to be done for the sake of our brands, so that they can compete globally. I am taking the initiative to push this need, and I will continue to push until something happens that will support the advancement of our brands.

I totally understand that there are many elements involved in market expansion. But if the proper planning does not start today, when will it start? Our consumers are wooed by foreign brands from across the globe; their confidence in imported brands is much stronger due to the effects of both brand presentation and global strategy. We must realize that if we don't initiate our moves today, we don't know when we will see a difference. The reason I address the CEO community about the importance of moving forward is that most CEOs are also business owners here in our region. They, not the teams behind them, are fully responsible for the life cycles of their brands. They decide on every move of the brand. It is a pity that at times a CEO may take things personally and disagree with his or her team based on personal reasons rather than on the total equity and best interests of his business. Such unprofessional behavior can never help us push our brands to their ultimate potential in this era of globalization.

I am arguing this case for the best interests of our region. We have the chance to see how to work with models and move away from being 100% interested in working just with brand agents of our own region. We can initiate a new goal: to search for agents who can represent our brands in their countries or across the globe.

I might sound angry here. I am angry, in a way, because I feel relatively powerless because I know I can do nothing as a single individual. I need every private sector business owner to invest a certain concern into his brand for the good of our region. I understand how important it is for global brands to exist in our region and I am all for that—but equal trade is better for the global market's needs, and it works to the benefit of our region, allowing us to enjoy the role of providers and not just of consumers.

Most of the companies that are operating in the region are dominant within their category and are the first to fill in the blanks and dominate, and in most cases fast-moving consumer goods (FMCG) are more competitive in markets in the region than most other industries. We lack innovation and for the same reason that we operate in only a few industries as locally produced companies leaving aside multinationals.

Many factors must be considered prior to making any meaningful change, although, as has been said, much of the change simply needs to be made in the mindsets of most CEOs qualified or unqualified operating most of the companies. I have seen top management plan a company's three-year plan and attend strategy sessions, and hardly any of them understood the steps to the strategy. As a matter of fact, most often the CEO is a delusional leader who has driven his company through several rounds of trial and error, and yet it seems that the shareholders are not aware of their operating rights as members of the board. Funnily enough most of these CEOs hate for anyone to challenge them on their wrong thoughts. I myself have put some people in some very uncomfortable situations simply by calling their attention to the most simple truths.

At one point I truly believed that the CEO problem could be a fatal disease for the nation's business. What did we have as a symbol of manufacturing pride other than what God has blessed us with? Self-interest has taken over much of the business in our region. When you think of Egypt in the past year prior to the revolution, the country's head of business pretty much operated those companies the same way that the former president operated the country, as a dictatorship. I love Egypt, and I have had great memories in that blessed country, and I hope that Egypt surmounts all its problems and thrives in great successes and becomes the producing hub of the Middle East and Africa. With the potential for change in the dawn of hope in Egypt, I have seen my own hope for change renewed.

The change that took place in Egypt is the voice of the people, and in much the same way the region's companies need a voice on the international front to present the great brands that future generations of the region can identify with and that will place us among the most competitive and successful growing regions in this century and in the centuries to come. I hope that the changes in our business behaviors and brands will help us lead the pack and bring our skillful youth to the front row of the modern age of industry.

All of us in the Arab business world need to take this auspicious time in the history of our people to think much more deeply about what's holding us back and why we seem to ignore reality and live in our own sheltered world, assuming that the business world is wrong and we are right. Did we measure our previous failures and find ways to build a solid foundation out of them? No, because we simply denied the force of the change taking us over because of our distress concerning our lack of control. Yet our allegiance to our nations has fallen short because the corner stone of self-interest has taken over the force of our thoughts as the reality of our self-driven society.

How do we conduct ourselves from here on? No one has the all the answers, and I fear that any small-scale suggestions may be rejected because they simply don't serve anyone's self-interest. So I say, bring on the revolution. Let the brand revolution begin that will put our products in the world market and eradicate the old habits of doing business, because most businesses have to change and be led by leaders who can add value to our markets. If the bums won't change, throw the bums out. Even if the bum is you.

I have endeavored to give several recommendations based on my position and my sense of duty, and yet I'll never enforce my opinion as your final solution. But these recommendations are born out of experiences I have had in the kingdom of Saudi Arabia and elsewhere in the region. Nothing about these recommendations is based on mere opinion, but on facts that if we face them will drive us closer to reality. But that's only if we want to face reality as it is. I know that few of us would willingly shy away from reality.

Facing the most simple truths, however, can be deeply transformative for a person or a company. That simple act can bring our future very much closer to success. One suggestion I have for anyone reading this book is as follows: Today, face something that's difficult for you to look at, with acceptance and openness. I'm not asking you to do anything about it, or bludgeon yourself with it, or do anything at all. Tomorrow, look at another thing you've been afraid to face. I think within a few days you might see your life and your business start to transform, simply by a daily practice of acknowledging things that are difficult to acknowledge.

Change Means the Youth Lead

The youth are the true engine of change for the business environment, and too few people are taking steps to support the youth in their life business endeavors. Why stop the change when it is here; why battle it because a few old folks are scared of the truth and would rather that everyone else pay the price for them to hold on to their seats as they battle the changes? Does facing some of the truths you have read here hurt? Let it! That pain might be one of the medicines for change. The way to seek change is to confront the truth and deal with it as a reality, in order to assess the required changes and drive for what's urgently needed.

For many years, I've seen a great many young people with amazing gifts and qualifications being driven by a few people who wish only to make their thoughts uniform. I have had firsthand experience of such behavior from a financial company I consulted with in the city of Jeddah, Saudi Arabia. The so-called executive director of the organization who seems to be the CEO is a corrupt individual. First and foremost, he hires only people who will agree with his views and not challenge him. Second, he seeks to create ways for his frontline to do most of the unethical work for him. Third, he has his wife working for him, qualified or not, as the head of a department. He has her there in order to benefit even more from the shareholders' money. Is that ethical? He fails to understand the role of the consultant and read a few chapters of *Blue Ocean Strategy* and decided that would be his strategy for the next few years. Apparently he took major steps to photocopy this book and distribute it to his management and staff to proceed in this great endeavor. The shareholders seem to fear this man's never-ending sagas and games. He has opened and closed branches of this company in just a few years. His international operations came to a complete halt after a few years of failure. A company with over $200,000,000 in investments started earning per annum an average of $3 million. He cut jobs left and right to show earnings, but failed even then to impress the shareholders.

Collective Responsibility

The success of a business is the collective responsibility of the owners, the employees and the business representation, and it is a matter of national pride for the global market. Better business conduct truly spreads across the board; it opens many gates for you as a shareholder, and for owners to facilitate opportunities for you and others. My recommendations are driven by a concern that even with the opportunities of emerging markets represented by the BRIC states and the T states, as well as the open gate of globalization, the MENA brands will not sustain their growth unless they act now and consider marketing as the core of their business and their support for all their business lines. If they fail to do so, the result will be catastrophic. Nothing will ever rescue these brands and their enormous investments unless a foreign buyout takes place—which is fine—it is part of the capitalistic world of trade.

I have made several major recommendations here—I'd like to briefly list a few more based on problems we've identified. First, no more chump change. Businesses must begin to transform themselves from being traders like our forefathers to real business people who accept the work, accept that the owner should be treated like an employee, and that whatever applies to all applies to the owner, too. Separate the company's and your personal needs, act like the leader, and do as the company requires and not according to your personal requirements.

Other Suggestions

Don't base your business on opinions but on well-researched facts, so that your decisions are balanced, led by conviction and factually sound, so that the world that you are managing is well suited to produce the ultimate brands.

Think about successful companies. Think about why so many Western and Far Eastern companies have excelled as they have, and how your business practices are different from theirs. Their success is based on their positive thinking and on the fact that the right to manage, listen and accept drove them to create, innovate and drive their brands across the world, and here in the MENA region when we failed to do so.

Consider your employees the biggest part of the work of performance enhancement. The improvement of any company pays that company back in building its strength and allowing it to continue performing competitively.

Adopt a corporate strategy. If you have never worked on a SWOT analysis, you can't draft a mission statement and vision. Too many people use the vision and mission statement merely as part of their corporate profile image, which means nothing to the direction in which their company is driven. You cannot plan to have a marketing strategy drafted if the fundamentals are not in place. Or let me say this: If you are advertising-oriented, how do you aim your advertising, and what impact can it have if the above questions are not answered?

Hire competent employees, including in your job. Who are your employees? What credentials do they have in terms of experience and education? If you hire no experienced employees or a few with experience from the CEO to the bottom front-liners, how will you initiate or achieve your goals? All the initiatives we've discussed here need to be executed by mid-management and bottom-liners, and for this reason it is highly imperative to hire employees who have a number of years of experience in the set field.

Cultivate unity in your company. The unity of the organization as a brand has great emotional attributes in terms of the perceptions of consumers and others, and these attributes must be well-managed by the human capital and marketing departments, and led by the CEO of the organization. The CEO is the leader who sets the example for others to follow. As I've mentioned, two great examples for me are the late Steve Jobs of Apple and Richard Branson of Virgin, both of whom led their brands well over the past two decades. Such examples should represent a great example and opportunity for regional CEOs to change how they run their businesses and how they lead.

Educate. I would argue that many of our problems have their start in our region at the university level. Most of the universities in the region do not offer marketing as a core major, but only as an extension of other majors. Then too, there is a lack of knowledge even in some parts of academia as to what marketing actually is.

Update. Technology is taking over all forms of change as more of our youth are being adapted to it or are adopted into it. No strategy for business will work that doesn't accommodate the power of the Internet and the power of information technology at a very fundamental level.

Globalize. In this era of globalization, major European, American and Asian firms are penetrating brands all over the world and even in our own neighborhoods. But we don't yet have the competitive edge to compete locally or even globally. Big organizations from abroad are implementing merger and acquisition strategies to expand their consumer base. Local firms appreciate these mergers because those brands are foreign-owned, have a proper global branding strategy, and are cash generators. Our local brands still fail to meet customer expectations and confidence, however. We must act *today* to brand our products, deployed with marketing applications, so that in the long term we may have a global competitive edge.

CEOs need to realize that Arabs are not the only consumers who might appreciate our brands! There are potential new customers all over the world. The target audiences exist, and you need only deploy proper strategies to reach them. The world, as we have heard constantly, is becoming a macro-market. To ensure our brands are not lost in the global market, we need to set short- and long-term strategies to move ahead. Be confident about your brand and let's move it forward.

Do your job. You should remember that you're always, as an employee, a foot soldier of the brand.

Chapter 12:
Messages

The following are some recommendations I would make to people in various titles, organizations and fields, if I could speak to them today. I take this opportunity to directly address most areas where marketing could change things for the better. My recommendations are straight from experience and not born from emotion, so my bluntness should not be taken as negative criticism, but as an attempt to provide a positive eye-opener.

To shareholders

When you first thought of investing, was it a trend you followed and in which you thought you would get a break? Was it because your friends joined in? What was it exactly that made you decide to invest in a given company? Was it the business plan? Did you look at the people behind the project? Was there strong managerial experience or just product development? Arguably there must have been something you witnessed and agreed on and saw as an opportunity. I hope that your investment was not based on your CFO's opinion, who pretty much gets any investments wrong in the long term. So as a shareholder, what was it? And on what did you base your assumptions? Did you look at the marketing forecast? All these questions are matters that you as a shareholder must answer prior to thinking of investing a penny in a business. My recommendation to you as a shareholder is as follows:

A. Before checking the business plan look at the body of the organization and who will be the key players. What is their managerial and leadership experience? Did they ever create business models and have they attained success? Look at these points first, because a company is not only about assets; it's about the people who will operate it.

B. Look at the business plan, and please don't run straight to the financials. First, look at each section of the seven properly, and formulate your questions about each of these sections in detail. Expect to be answered fully on each of your questions, and not half-heartedly. Please make sure you have your own board of advisors and make sure there is a professional marketing advisor on the team.

C. Ask for a complete fold plan for marketing and make sure that it contains a strategically competitive edge both in the short term and long term.

D. Require the prospective organizational chart and a simple draft of the possible corporate strategy, because the externals of the corporate strategy reflect strongly on the possible draft of the marketing strategy.

E. Examine the prospective in terms of who will be the potential CEO. What is his ability to manage by objectives rather than to manage an overall process? Objectives do drive strategies into results.

F. Finally, don't decide on the investment unless you can do so democratically, without any form of favoritism. Make sure your advisors have collectively agreed on all aspects of the investment.

To Business owners

Usually business owners in our region run their own businesses whether they are experienced or not. They are in small to mid-size businesses and frequently their investments are horrendous. For example I know of a person who invested close to $4 million US on a restaurant—a restaurant that had no drafted plan of long-term expansion. I found that amazing. In our region there is no concept of "start small and mature your business." It is "start big and take a picture next to it and advertise it to family and friends." Usually this size of business as a startup drafts hardly any business plans or even any paperwork. It consists of an idea implanted with the thought of buying and selling without any thought of structured processing. Some do make it through, but these are also faced eventually with restructuring their current situation and that process gets costly. Some make major mistakes in the structuring process. I am one of the supporters of small and midsize companies. By far they make up the largest portion of any economy. But I would also like to recommend that these companies should follow established guidelines or hire a business consultant in the beginning phases to reduce the likelihood of overwhelming crises that they might face both financially and organizationally.

It is my concern that small businesses should receive the utmost care and support in setting up. I also believe that most chambers of commerce can provide the right tools and information they need, but again most start-ups fail to take even the initiative to investigate and take the right steps. I am sorry, but the fact is that some of these owners are taken in by the ego of being a know-it-all until they fall on their faces. My recommendation applies for small businesses much more to others due to the fact that they need to be well guided in all their business practices. Some fail, but even those who fail can succeed tomorrow. In any case, accepting the truth and taking the right steps and keeping the ego at home or in the closet will be the beginning of any successes. Great ideas are frequently born from small businesses, which then become big businesses. Every great idea has a home, but it also has a start.

Not all great ideas are workable ideas. They need to be modeled by experts and tested in order to be or become workable ideas. As a small business owner, you should always put yourself in the shoes of your potential customer and see their needs and expectations and build accordingly. Avoid the personal test, because you're just an individual in the midst of a huge population. For small businesses to constantly do market research may be cost-prohibitive. If so, meet your customers and hear directly from them what they like and what they like to see. That can be your in-house research. Collecting all this data regularly and building your product and communication accordingly, you're moving in the right direction, because such work is based on your consumer's observations and not your own, or your friends' or family's. The list of my recommendations for small business is as follows.

To CEOs

I am speaking to the professional CEOs in the region with track records of successful business ventures in the region. I am speaking to CEOs who are visionaries and who wish to do something with the company they are operating today. My message to you is, please make the difference so that we can see our brands competitive in the global markets. Please make sure that we have brands that will penetrate the world market and keep us competitive. If you decided to be a professional CEO, then you've had the experience of operating a company on some scale and you know the responsibilities that your shareholders have placed on your shoulders. You need to deliver as required and not just to suit your personal vision and needs as most CEOs still do. Please move away from the title and roll up your sleeves and run into the frontline and set an example to those who will follow you. Make sure that everyone in the company from the office boy to the vice president knows you in person and not just through a picture.

Ask your CMO (Chief Marketing Officer) to walk you through the department and have you see what your customers think of your company. Make sure that you revisit the marketing strategy to see that it is aligned with your corporate strategy. Ask to see it quite often, and please visit the numbers and ask for reasoning.

Make sure to make it a habit to visit your frontline every now and then to ask them about the company culture and values. Ask them what the company brand stands for and see if they know. Make sure that you don't build divisions in the company or team and make sure the company is free of gossip, and for those that gossip, alert them of your plan. Make sure that the overall company system and policies are well addressed to everyone. Keep them in mind all the time, and not only below your line of managers. Remember that an organization's unity lives in the heart of every employee that will love his job and strive to outperform your competitors.

Keep it simple, because your line of managers and staff comes from all walks of life. Even if you are all from the same company, remember that just a simple thought counts. You as a leader of the organization are supposed to set the example for all and lead each one of them to the next step. Your management and staff need to look up to you and admire your work so that they call follow the same path and so that the company is consistent in its management and approach. There are world-class CEOs that have set examples globally, but there are few of Arab origin except some who are Western educated and are driven to change their organization. Ask yourself: Where do you stand? How would you be able to manage the expectations and listen more than speak and learn firsthand from those who know more than you in your domain. Do you care? Find out the reason for other people's successes and avoid the inferiority complex that has caused many of the regional CEOs to be doomed from the start.

Get ready to swim against the waves and challenge the status quo. Tolerate things that you think you won't tolerate when you need to do so. Offer training courses and workshops to your staff so that they can appreciate and do more for the company. Change your staff's mindset from that of employees to that of creative thinkers, so that they can add value to the company and push forward with the rest of the team. A few things to consider are, why did shareholders choose you to be the CEO of this company? Because they thought you were well skilled and able to attain the stated goals. Therefore, that responsibility is supposed to be on your shoulders. These are the recommendations I would give any CEO who cares to work for the benefit of the company and not for his own personal preferences. It is critically important to consider the many challenges that you might face and consider them to be positive in all cases. Consider that the shareholders' trust can be earned only once, and not several times.

To Governments

You are responsible for the national economy. It is up to you to build the proper policies that will govern the interests of each citizen. You are the lawmakers who can help the small and midsize companies flourish and prosper, but any sort of law needs to bring with it a commission that will govern the initiative. Most small and midsize businesses fail to head to a responsible hub to address their concerns. For this reason a number of businesses at the entrepreneurial level tend to fold before they are able to witness the heyday of their projects. Therefore, if governments in the Middle East are charging the public with many business initiatives, they need to support such initiatives with laws able to secure small businesses from being hijacked by the financially well-settled companies.

Good laws can reduce the amount of anger and stop the great number of bright ideas from migrating from the region. Many of our great ideas have materialized elsewhere as a source of great pride for the creator and the nation that adopted him. The regional governments must adopt a strategy to intake all these great ideas and have a hub to drive them into a business pipeline that is governed by laws and systems.

So what should governments do? They should build independent agencies that report to a ministry. The agency should be the force that will be the regulator and governing body, and not the project provider. In most cases government agencies like to hold everything that concerns them and some things that don't, and that's the reality of our region.

To Citizens

It is fully the responsibility of every citizen to ask for their right to the value paid for the brands they desire. If citizens of all nations feel deceived by owners of brands, they should protest such products and let authorities in the local government know of any incidents. You as citizens and loyal buyers of the brands you love must protest and stand for the brands you love if you see any unwanted changes taking place in the management. These brands are created for you and much research has been done to study your behavior and needs and determine how to create and model this brand for you. If the company has invested this much effort, then the brand at the end of the day is your brand, and you are the champion of this brand to sustain its existence. As citizens of these countries and as loyal brand followers you should inquire with the companies about any sudden changes that have taken place. Whether you're in New York, Bangkok, London, Paris, Tokyo, Cairo, Dubai or anywhere else in the world, these brands that have targeted you for so long and have spoken to you are yours to control when you think they are in danger. Ask for what's your right, and most companies in the Western nations will respond to complaints instantaneously because they know and believe that their brands belong to you. So keep in mind that you should ask for what's yours, or else what you purchased is not the brand that you've loved, and you don't care for its fate.

To Entrepreneurs

Have you ever asked yourself what it is that you wish to do? Did you ever ask yourself how you wish to do it? What is your long-term vision? These are questions you should ask yourself prior to starting your new venture. There are many elements you must consider when you think of your new venture. One of the most important things to consider is product. What is it to be? How do you plan to develop this product and protect it? Look at all the legal issues that pertain to your country's business laws. Hire a lawyer who will assist you in addressing all your legal issues prior to developing your little venture.

I would recommend that you develop a system for your new organization so that you will be able to manage your objectives and drive your products much more easily to end users. One thing you must consider at this stage of your business is that the customer is the key factor, and your organization should be all about customers inside and out, so that you are able to sustain growth and have repeat customers and cultivate loyalty to your newly created brands. Make sure that you focus and serve within the boundaries of your organizational ability, and do not expand more than expected. In most cases starters think by reducing their prices they will win customers. That's a wrong thought to cling to. Once you enter the price war, you won't be able to compete. Keep your offering reasonable to the product and service and focus on eventual increases per year. I have always recommended to small businesses that they consider referral and word of mouth as their primary tools of communication to spread and build their product reputation.

The concern of starting entrepreneurs in most cases is marketing lapses, and that should not be a concern if you have thought strategically prior to launching your new venture. Did you differentiate from your competition? Do you know who your audience is? Did you define the need? Did you build the new brand in its entirety from name to visual features to industry standards? These are questions to consider when starting your business, and not down the line when you've left bad impressions on your customers, which are almost impossible to move once imprinted. Keep in mind that your customers are the ones who will bring up your business, and at the same time one bad experience with them can bring it down. So marketing truly relies on what you plan to do prior to creating the engagement with your customers. If you fail to develop a strategy followed by planning the original thought, then consumer perception will not rise to expectations. The problem with all startups in the Middle East is the lack of laws concerning startups that will oversee the guiding laws to ensure their stability and protect them and their patents.

The motivational force for these startups in most cases is money and confidence. Especially in a region where most thoughts have been controlled or programmed there is less of a reason for anyone to move forward and start turning their thoughts to a model that will work well for them. Fear is another factor. Most grow up under house rules that are full of fear and under strict social rules which incline them to think it's all about sticking to the rules, which in my case I call controlling rules. For this reason and many others, regional young entrepreneurs fail to achieve their goals, and they live under constant pressure. These fundamentals must change from the grass roots of society, and the environment that this society operates in. We must keep in mind that without proper space, these youth will fail to operate correctly, and along with the governing body they will be misguided. We must have regulators, and these regulators should be business operators, as in many of the cases I have witnessed.

What is your objection?

My objective in this book has been to raise awareness of how important brands are and how they should be treated. In most cases CEOs and management in the Arab world look at brands from a cosmetic aspect and not in terms of the essence of the brand. Often, products are only built to become brands in a cosmetic sense, such as through logos, pictures, design and content, and not through the brand life. In most cases companies face execrable failure if they take such an approach, and they come to fold sooner rather than later.

I know that my subject is only a portion of a company's potential problems, but I can only addresses within my field of expertise. The pattern of cosmetic brand building is a pattern that seems to be embraced by many, and yet the consumer is left with confusion as to what the brand stands for. For this reason most brands decline from their day of inception. I have taken the liberty, and have not faced a law suit, of keeping an endless list of them. Most in the region were cases of CEOs running their companies like dictators. I am sure it should be that the ministries of trade in the respective countries should protect the national industry from becoming extinct. If we look at the major world stock markets, we'll see that most companies that are trading are reputable brands, yet within the Middle East this necessity of a good reputation is ignored, as the stock markets here are a fraction of the size of the world-class stock markets. This is another indicator that the truth of the necessity of change seems to be only vaguely understood or ignored by special interests who wish to keep their jobs, and by shareholders who seem to fear change and would rather sit in their comfort zones.

It has been over ten years since I have started raising my concerns on this subject, and I have written numerous articles for local publications, such as *The Gulf Marketing Review* and through the social media and on my personal blog. It has been my deep concern and life quest to see the change that will help the region to be fruitful with its local brands, and to build world admiration, and for national brands to appear in the world media and be followed by millions of regional brand lovers. Take for example most of the US or European brands. Even those great nations are built as brands and as destinations for millions, whether for business, leisure, education or even immigration. If my case doesn't appeal to the mass audience, that is fine, but my case is the reality of my domain as a brand marketing strategy consultant. Even the way we used to conduct marketing forty years ago has changed until today.

Chapter 13:
Conclusion

The needful change must come now, or the result could be catastrophic for the region. The political change of the Arab spring has achieved its primary goal, which was to get rid of the regional dictators who clung to power by force. The second revolution should be a business revolution, to eradicate the useless CEOs and Executive Directors who are harming our business environment and who fail to understand the importance of brands for the company cash flow and for the national pride.

If the region is to grow, it is vitally important that these changes occur soon, or again we will fall a century behind the rest of the world, as the case is now. The failure of the region to progress will be determined based on its economic and political standing. At the same time the culture simmers on the front burners, and this dilemma must come to an end. If ever there will be a time to change it is now. The region cannot wait another ten to fifteen years; it should align itself with the rest of the world and tap into the worldwide changes, and capitalize on the opportunities that are appearing within the hands of so many. We must also change the educational system so that it serves the coming generations and the generations thereafter. These changes must take place immediately so that they may serve the business environment and lead us into the future, so that we can be one of the major trends on the global front.

We must lead so as to bring forth the great changes we have needed for so long, and to make room for the new generation to put their thoughts into action and lead our businesses into the world market. We must remove ourselves from the patterns we've been following for too long, mixing our business with our traditions and culture rather than keeping our business independent from our home and family habits. The current majority of CEOs of this region when it comes to marketing support are useless. They put on a front as if they know, or even seem half knowledgeable, but the truth remains veiled. I have seen and consulted numerous companies in which the CEO or the business owners are the major reasons for the failure, but they have failed to admit the truth so that they can improve. This saga has continued until the businesses completely shut down. These stories I have experienced have been repeated many times across the region.

Most CEOs and business owners tend to repeat the stories of their forefathers and continue in the same patterns, believing the story will succeed as it did back in the good old days. Each age's nature differs from the other and the nature of this age leads us to believe that we must innovate to lead; we must change our behavior and embrace change as it comes and pave the way for the young to lead our destiny. If all these changes and a few more occur, then we will be able to secure the future of generations still to come who are depending on us to do so, and that sort of change should be considered in order to sustain growth.

In this book I have shared my thoughts for myself and for whoever reads this book, and I plan to spread its message across the web or even through traditional media. We must raise our voices to change how we do business, and we must consider appointing governing bodies that will protect and guide these business and commissions, and regulators who will hold the law in process. I urge those of you with bright minds not to run your businesses the way your fathers and forefathers did. Our young people must have room to think and to operate freely, and lead their independent thoughts into action in the real world. I support the youth because they will lead our brands into the future and into the global market. Unless this is done then we can consider that our woeful patterns will continue to repeat themselves. Ask for what you believe in and do what you intend to do, and save the region from its business failures starting now. Let the change begin.

This should be a revolution of brands, and brands should take over traditional marketing or trade marketing. Brands are the preeminent form of marketing in any strong competitive market, and only brands can achieve the ultimate goals that this region seeks. Only our brands will help our nations to be branded in turn, and help our communities to flourish so that we can lure the world to us and have them experience our business, our culture and our traditions.

Brands change nations and build nations. No nation on this earth has branded itself better than the United States of America. America is a great brand that its citizens look up to, as does the rest of the world. America's brand is built from its essence, and delivered for the world to experience. Other potent brands among nations are France, Spain and Italy, each of which has branded itself for its own unique purposes. France and Italy are leaders in fashion and Spain in sea leisure.

The greatness of a nation is in its brand, and in what it promises to deliver and provide—a single experience that will make its citizen proud. To be loyal to your country is to be loyal to the brand that was created to serve its people. Bring on the change and change how the Middle East will be in the years to come, especially the region's businesses which have been operated by dictator CEOs who are too selfish to give up their posts for the incoming generation to have an opportunity to lead. What do we wish the brand of the Middle East to be associated with? I would suggest that we should not wait on political leaders or protestors, or anyone else, to make that new face of our nation a reality. Middle Eastern businesses have the power, the money, and the vision to give the region a new, beautiful face to the world. All that's needed is the vision and the hard work, the will and the courage, but also the honesty and humility, to do what each of us can do to begin to build something real.